MARKETING PLANNING
AND
COMPETITIVE STRATEGY

EUGENE J. KELLEY, editor

The Pennsylvania State University

PRENTICE-HALL FOUNDATIONS OF MARKETING SERIES

CONSUMER BEHAVIOR
HAROLD H. KASSARJIAN   *University of California*
PETER D. BENNETT *The Pennsylvania State University*

MARKETING MANAGEMENT AND THE BEHAVIORAL ENVIRONMENT
PERRY BLISS *State University of New York at Buffalo*

MEN, MOTIVES, AND MARKETS
WROE ALDERSON
MICHAEL H. HALBERT

QUANTITATIVE METHODS IN MARKETING
RONALD E. FRANK and PAUL E. GREEN *University of Pennsylvania*

PRICING DECISIONS AND MARKETING POLICY
KRISTIAN PALDA *Queens University*

PRODUCT POLICY AND STRATEGY
DAVID J. LUCK *Southern Illinois University*

PROMOTION: A BEHAVIORAL VIEW
HARPER W. BOYD, JR. *Stanford University*
SIDNEY J. LEVY *Northwestern University*

SALES MANAGEMENT
JOSEPH W. THOMPSON *Michigan State University*

CHANNEL MANAGEMENT
REAVIS COX and THOMAS SCHUTTE *University of Pennsylvania*

MARKETING LOGISTICS
BERNARD J. LALONDE *Ohio State University*

ORGANIZATIONAL BUYING BEHAVIOR
FREDERICK E. WEBSTER, JR. *Dartmouth College*
YORAM WIND *University of Pennsylvania*

INTERNATIONAL MARKETING   second edition
JOHN FAYERWEATHER *New York University*

MARKETING AND PUBLIC POLICY
E. T. GRETHER *University of California*

MARKETING IN THE CANADIAN ENVIRONMENT
B. E. MALLEN *Sir George Williams University*

CASES IN MARKETING MANAGEMENT
EDWARD C. BURSK *Harvard University*

ADVANCED CASES IN MARKETING MANAGEMENT
EDWARD C. BURSK and STEPHEN A. GREYSER *Harvard University*

HISTORY OF MARKETING
STANLEY C. HOLLANDER *Michigan State University*

CONTEMPORARY ISSUES IN MARKETING
EUGENE J. KELLEY *The Pennsylvania State University*

MARKETING PLANNING AND COMPETITIVE STRATEGY
EUGENE J. KELLEY *The Pennsylvania State University*

PRENTICE-HALL FOUNDATIONS OF MARKETING SERIES

PRENTICE-HALL, INC., Englewood Cliffs, New Jersey

MARKETING PLANNING AND COMPETITIVE STRATEGY

EUGENE J. KELLEY

The Pennsylvania State University

MARKETING PLANNING AND COMPETITIVE STRATEGY
EUGENE J. KELLEY
The Pennsylvania State University

PRENTICE-HALL, INC., Englewood Cliffs, New Jersey

FOUNDATIONS OF MARKETING SERIES

Printed in the United States of America

Library of Congress
Catalog Card No.: 70–170039

13–558304–7

Current printing (last digit)
10   9   8   7   6   5   4   3   2

Prentice-Hall International, Inc., *London*
Prentice-Hall of Australia, Pty., Ltd., *Sydney*
Prentice-Hall of Canada, Ltd., *Toronto*
Prentice-Hall of India Private Limited, *New Delhi*
Prentice-Hall of Japan, Inc., *Tokyo*

FOUNDATIONS
OF
MARKETING SERIES

The Foundations of Marketing is a series of authoritative and concise books prepared to serve the need for teaching materials incorporating the results of recent research and developments in the study and practice of marketing. The structure of the series—its flexibility within unity of purposes—enables the teacher to construct a complete basic marketing course, adjustable to a level of rigor of the teacher's choosing. Certain or all books can be combined to accomplish individual course objectives. Individual books are self-contained, reasonably complete treatments of the fundamental changes taking place in their areas. Students have the benefits of being introduced to the managerial approach to the field and to the socioeconomic process of marketing by authorities actively engaged in study and research in each field.

An overview of the series and of the managerial approach to marketing is provided by

Marketing Planning and Competitive Strategy

Four books treat important aspects of scientific methodology and decision making in marketing:

Consumer Behavior
Marketing Management and the Behavioral Environment
Men, Motives, and Markets
Quantitative Methods in Marketing

Key policy areas of marketing are covered in

Pricing Decisions and Marketing Policy
Product Policy and Strategy
Promotion: A Behavioral View

Sales Management
Channel Management
Marketing Logistics
Organizational Buying Behavior

Important environmental areas in marketing are emphasized in

International Marketing
Marketing and Public Policy
Marketing in the Canadian Environment

All books may profitably use as supplements

Contemporary Issues in Marketing
Cases in Marketing Management
Advanced Cases in Marketing Management
History of Marketing

It is hoped that the series will stimulate independent and intelligent thought about the central issues of marketing analysis and policy and that readers will find the books useful guides to a creative and disciplined approach to meeting complex and changing marketing problems.

EUGENE J. KELLEY, *Editor*

I would like to thank Gilbert D. Harrell, James O. Johnson, John T. Redington, Ronald R. Socha, Thomas J. Steele, and Lewis R. Tucker, Jr., doctoral candidates at The Pennsylvania State University, for their assistance in the development of this book. I am also indebted to Miss Brenda D. Nyman for her help in preparing the manuscript for publication.

CONTENTS

PART ONE
MARKETING AND
THE MANAGEMENT OF CHANGE

1

MARKETING POLICY AND SYSTEMS   1

The Field of Marketing   1
Marketing as the Foundation of Competitive Policy   5
Marketing as a Discipline   11
The Systems Approach   12
Marketing's Broader Dimensions   12
Metamarketing: A New Approach   13
Effective Marketing Orientation—The Marketing Concept   15

2

INFORMATION AND SYSTEMS MANAGEMENT IN MARKETING   17

Marketing and Change   19
Marketing in an Information Society   20
Knowledge Areas Underlying Marketing Decisions   21

PART TWO
THE MANAGEMENT PROCESS
IN MARKETING

3

MARKETING OPPORTUNITY ASSESSMENT   33

Entrepreneurial-Decision Functions   33
Assessment of Marketing Opportunity   35
External Environments of Marketing   38
Analysis of Environmental Forces   39
Market Segmentation   48

4

MARKETING PLANNING FOR THE FIRM   52

Planning: The Basis of Marketing Management   52
Social System Orientation to Business Planning   54
Innovation in Marketing Planning   61
Trends in Planning   64

5

ORGANIZATION AND CONTROL
OF THE MARKETING EFFORT   65

Development of Marketing Organizations in Manufacturing Firms   65
From a Production to a Marketing Orientation   66
A Systems View of Organization   73
Control: A Systems View   74
Organization and Control: Planning Perspectives   76

PART THREE
MANAGING THE
MARKETING MIX

6

PRODUCT POLICY AND THE MARKET OFFERING   80

Product Policy   81
Pricing Policy   91

7

PROMOTION AND DISTRIBUTION POLICIES   97

Promotion Policy   97
Distribution Policy   108

PART FOUR
MARKETING'S
BROADER HORIZONS

8

INTEGRATING MARKETING IN ENVIRONMENTS OF UNCERTAINTY   115

Integrating the Field of Marketing   116
Environmental Management and Socio-marketing   120
Marketing Audit   121
International Marketing   122
Broadening Market Applications   123
Professionalism and Marketing Education   124

MARKETING POLICY AND SYSTEMS

Changes in marketing in recent years have come at such an accelerated rate that the field can be described as the "new marketing." This book provides a framework for the analysis of changing business and social marketing problems and opportunities in the context of the emerging "new marketing."

Marketing includes four interrelated evolving segments: *managerial, scientific, institutional,* and *societal.* Each segment is broader and more specialized than conventional wisdom suggests because each is broader and more specialized than at any time in the past. The basic viewpoint of this book focuses on the managerial aspects of marketing in business firms. Understanding of the managerial approach is important to those with specialized interest in other segments of marketing. The manager must also understand the other approaches: marketing management is essentially an integrative activity involving the combining of scientific, institutional, and sociotechnological inputs to achieve marketing goals in business and nonbusiness institutions.

The Field of Marketing

As seen in Fig. 1-1, the four segments in the marketing field are bounded both by the environment and by the limits imposed by the perceptions of the observer. In some companies marketing is still concerned with little more than sales force and advertising management; in other firms marketing is an integrative corporate activity that provides the direction for corporate strategic planning. In non-business organizations executives are only beginning to perceive the potential of marketing in achieving institutional goals. The difference between these approaches is due in part to the perceptions of management and its attitudes toward change.

The consumer has long been central in marketing thought and practice. The "Customer is King" is not a new marketing concept. What is new in marketing thought is increased recognition of the view that service to customers involves not only satisfying individual consumers but also fulfilling environmental and social concerns. The entire field of marketing, therefore, revolves around understanding and serving the buyer in his dual role of consumer-citizen.

As indicated by the arrows in Fig. 1–1, marketing is characterized by interaction and information exchange between segments. Central to the entire field is the *consumer-citizen* to whom the activities of marketing are directed. This is not merely an altruistic view, for the consumer-citizen possesses veto power, by his purchase or non-purchase decision, over all

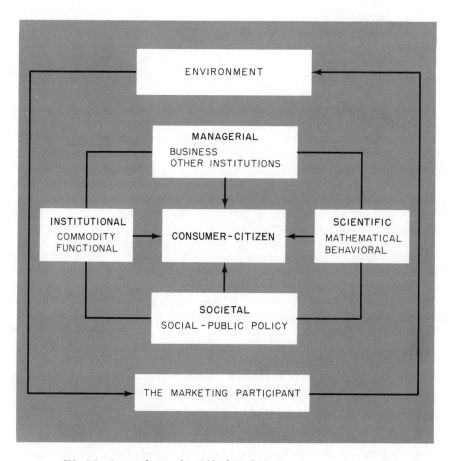

FIG. 1-1 Approaches to the Field of Marketing

Figure 1-1 indicates the four major approaches to the field of marketing, which all focus on the problems of serving the consumer-citizen. All approaches are made within the constraints of environmental conditions and the problem-solving capacities, interests, and abilities of the marketing participant.

efforts of business to serve him at a profit. The consumer-citizen, as a member of the larger society beyond the family unit, also holds political power over the corporation.

As suggested by the fourfold segmentation of the field, there is no single answer to the question, "What is Marketing?" Marketing is a multivariate process whose inputs and outputs reflect the tangible and intangible influences of society and the business enterprise as a whole. Therefore, this book emphasizes conceptual understanding of problems rather than the techniques of marketing management problem-solving, while also recognizing the importance of knowledge accumulation in the many fields of learning which influence marketing theories and practice.

In emphasizing a business-oriented view of marketing two basic questions arise: (1) What is a business? and (2) What is marketing's role in the business? While there are many answers to these questions, Peter Drucker has provided one which is particularly apt for marketers: "Business is a process which converts a resource, distinct knowledge, into a contribution of economic value in the marketplace. The purpose of a business is to create a customer." [1] A business which defines its purpose in these terms inevitably recognizes the importance of customer-satisfying functions in reaching growth and profit goals. The profitable satisfaction of consumer needs becomes the prime management task for marketing and non-marketing executives alike.

Corporate profit and growth in a market society depends on effective marketing. Marketing is delegated the mission of performing those business tasks leading to customer satisfactions and resulting corporate profit through the development and distribution of customer-satisfying goods and services. This charge requires performance of business activities needed to identify the needs and wants of particular market segments, to guide and deliver a flow of want-satisfying goods and services from production to consumption, and to maintain and expand customer markets for this flow. From a managerial viewpoint, then, marketing knowledge provides direction for corporate planning and operations.

Of course, there are dimensions of marketing other than the managerial. The legal perspective focuses upon the nature of the exchange function or the "transaction." In the economic sense, marketing deals with the adjustment of supply and demand by influencing buyer-seller relationships and facilitating the transfer of demand-satisfying goods and services. The social dimensions, while perhaps the most difficult to place in perspective, concern the total effectiveness of the marketing process in relation to the standard of living obtained by the society; the fact that marketing influences the "life-style" of customers indicates how important it is on the societal level.

As a summary definition, marketing is a social, economic and managerial process focused on the creation and delivery of want-satisfying ideas,

---

[1] Peter F. Drucker, *Managing for Results* (New York: Harper & Row, Publishers, 1964), p. 91. Drucker first defined the purpose of business as customer creation in his *Practice of Management* (1954).

goods and services.[2] The bases of effective marketing are identifying changing consumption requirements and managing organizational efforts required to supply ideas, goods and services to consumers. Marketing also includes the study of demand-generating, temporal, spatial, and environmental forces influencing market transactions and the interacting efforts and consumption responses of sellers and buyers.

It is difficult to convey in any formal definition the challenge and dynamism which are the dominant characteristics of contemporary marketing in a competitive environment. The essential managerial requirement for achievement, therefore, is a creative and innovative approach to market affairs. In this chapter the study of marketing problems begins with analysis of environmental changes and of concepts and systems which provide the basis of marketing opportunity and corporate service to the consumer-citizen.

The chapters in this book are organized as a sequence of activities, as indicated by the arrangement in Fig. 1–2. This chapter appraises marketing as a business and social process. Chapter 2, treating marketing and the knowledge explosion, provides an orientation to the analysis of knowledge which is relevant to marketing decision-making. Chapter 3 describes the task of assessing environmental and marketing opportunity. In Chapter 4 the corporate and market planning process is treated, and this is followed in Chapter 5 by a discussion of organization and control in marketing. Chapters 6 and 7 present materials on the marketing mix of a firm and consider various product, price, promotion, and distribution policies. In Chapter 8 a summarizing perspective is presented and some possible future lines of development in marketing are discussed. For purposes of simplicity, Fig. 1–2 does not show feedback. This notion and other systems concepts are introduced later.

Marketing as the Foundation of Competitive Policy

The one certainty about the environment in which business operates is that it is characterized by accelerating change. The social landscape of the developing environment is vastly different from the environmental landscape which is familiar to most of us, and on which most business theories and operating practices are based. Drucker has identified the major discontinuities, or changes in direction, which are important to those concerned with understanding marketing problems and opportunities;[3] his points may be summarized as follows:

New technologies are moving business to the early stages of a new era of innovation. Changes in information technology, for

[2] An older definition of marketing "as the delivery of a standard of living" is still useful. Paul M. Mazur, "Does Distribution Cost Enough?" *Fortune,* xxxvi (November 1947), 138.

[3] Peter F. Drucker, *The Age of Discontinuity* (New York: Harper & Row, Publishers, 1968), pp. ix–x.

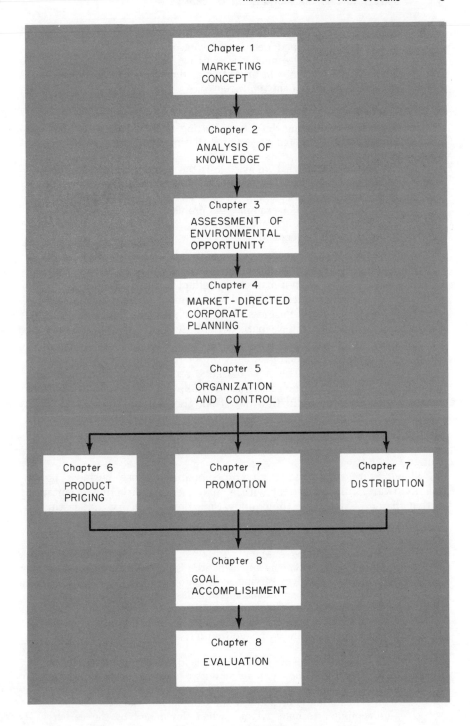

FIG. 1-2 Chapter Organization: A Marketing Planning Overview

example, are already fundamentally altering marketing and business planning and decision making.

The international economy is evolving into a "world" economy. Much of the change is in marketing as the world becomes one market—"one global shopping center."

A new sociopolitical reality of pluralistic institutions is developing and is rapidly changing the existing social and political matrix. Marketers are having difficulty adjusting to the new relationship among institutions—big government, business and other large institutions.

The recognition that knowledge is the "central capital, the cost center, and the crucial resource of the economy" is the most important change. Managing the efforts of the knowledge worker is becoming critical. For example, the problem of integrating the efforts of specialists in marketing and in research and development is not yet well understood.

Under such conditions of environmental change, it is no longer sufficient to define a business or even a market in product terms. Rather, a definition of the enterprise congruent with rapid environment change and innovative marketing should underlie business philosophy and practice. For example, during the 1970s major new markets will develop. These will include societal markets in which corporate marketing effort will be directed to selling systems to solve social problems rather than simply selling products to individual customers. The new markets, requiring creative marketing approaches, will include such fields as air pollution, water pollution, solid wastes management, public transportation, thermal pollution, and noise control. It is through the analysis of such environmental opportunities and the development of marketing policies that management responds to the pressures and opportunities presented by environmental and business change.

Following are examples of growth companies whose business policy definitions are truly congruent with a fundamental marketing orientation in that they are "daring in their innovation, broad in scope and lasting in execution."

Minnesota Mining & Manufacturing began with as lackluster a product line in its time as any of hundreds of smaller companies, with natural abrasives serving a declining market. Yet, to oversimplify, the company defined its business not as abrasives but as surface coatings, and from this definition have come products as wide-ranging as pressure-sensitive tape, roofing granules, carbonless copy paper, infrared image transfer, indeed over 30,000 such diverse products.

IBM began in the office equipment field, when it could barely be called a market. The company saw its market as tools and systems for the handling of information, not as paper or hardware as such. Such a definition later allowed the company to pioneer systems plus computer technology and, when threatened by the earlier introduction of a competitor's computer, to recognize the interrelation of the two and build the great service system which in 1967 had given the company over 75% of the computer market.

Xerox began with a rather narrow technology and, with some good fortune, developed the Xerographic method of copy reproduction, still the leading technology in this area. Yet the company does not view itself as an office copy machine manufacturer, but rather as a leader in graphic communications in information handling. In part because of this definition, it is a good bet that this great growth company, with present sales and earnings keyed to xerographic reproduction, will be in business and moving forward long after today's workhorse, the 914 office copier, has become obsolete.[4]

Each of these companies has developed a broad marketing foundation sufficiently flexible for adapting to change. Such foundations are basic to marketing leadership in a dynamic environment.

COMPETITION

Marketing executives in the United States operate in an affluent, competitive, consumption-oriented society. The marketing executive is no longer operating in an environment characterized by scarcity which assures a profitable market for his firm's products. More often than not, he finds the market he has developed and sold to successfully in the past drifting away from him. Competition has become more rigorous, as customer wants and needs become greater and more complete.

The nature of competition in contemporary business is illustrated by the fact that IBM and Xerox were originally in separate fields—IBM in data processing and Xerox in copying machines. These firms are now entering into direct competition. Xerox acquired a computer manufacturer, Scientific Data Systems, for nearly a billion dollars of stock. In Spring 1970 IBM introduced its first copying machine. One reason for this new competitiveness is that both companies changed their definitions of their corporate missions from missions defined in product terms to missions defined in terms of being in the information business. As C. Peter McColough, Xerox President, puts it:

> Xerox and IBM are the two big companies exclusively in the information business. IBM owns the manipulative data processing part, and we own a part that puts things on paper. But the lines of separation are getting blurred and it will be harder and harder to distinguish them. Sometime in the 1970's, we intend to be able to say to any big customer, "We can handle all your information needs." [5]

[4] Dan W. Lufkin, "Investing for Growth," in *The Anatomy of Wall Street*, ed. Charles J. Rolo and George J. Nelson (New York: Award Books, 1969), p. 132.

[5] "Two Gee-Whiz Giants Go At Each Other," *Business Week* (June 13, 1970), pp. 70–71ff.

This blurring of competive lines is widespread and has implications for market-oriented definitions for the business enterprise. In the search for customer-satisfying goods and services and concomitant growth and profit, a firm generates new concepts of purpose in response to changing environmental and competitive conditions.

PROFITS AND CUSTOMER SATISFACTIONS

The challenge of modern business is to accomplish the objectives of profitable creation and sale of products and services by providing customer satisfactions while maintaining a proper and strong social posture. This is why "Marketing, in the fullest sense of the word, is the name of the game." [6] Tradeoffs between these objectives are often necessary in modern business. For example, one way to increase customer satisfactions might be to sell the product below cost. However, the firm needs profits to survive and it is management's responsibility to obtain the profits necessary for survival and growth. The task of planning toward profit objectives is growing increasingly complex as the social objective of the business enterprise and of marketing is assuming more importance. In the short run social responsibility often seems to conflict with the profit motive.

Marketing, in its broadest sense, is the social instrumentality through which the material goods and culture of a society are transmitted to its members. Because of its importance marketing has *social* as well as economic goals. The social nature of marketing is one reason the field is being reconceptualized as a social process concerned with identifying and satisfying social as well as economic wants in the marketplace. The social process perspective contributes a vital and dynamic sense of direction to marketing.

SOCIAL RESPONSIBILITY

The social aspects of marketing are becoming increasingly important. Rising consumer expectations, concern for environmental issues, consumerism, and changing public sentiment toward marketing are influencing marketing policy. By its nature and by the system within which it operates, marketing serves a social function. Any society has two major marketing-related problems which it must deal with in meeting the material needs of its members. First, society must find a means of efficiently distributing and allocating goods in order to maximize want satisfaction. Marketing is a universal process which performs that function. Secondly, the business community does not live in a vacuum but is part of a total socioeconomic system. Business, as part of that system, is responsible for the efficient operation of the system. Thus, an ethical dimension as well as an inherent

---

[6] Robert Townsend, *Up the Organization* (New York: Alfred A. Knopf, Inc., 1970), p. 105.

dimension exists. The needs of customers, employees, and the resource environment are closely interrelated with the business community and become logically a part of its responsibility.

In the United States, business views on social responsibility have passed, in this century, through three phases characterized by distinct orientations to ethical problems in marketing and management.

The *legalistic* orientation is one in which the rules of the marketplace are determined by the law. This approach was dominant in the early twentieth century when power tended to be concentrated in the hands of a relatively small group of decision-makers. The major business goal was profit maximization with little or no thought being given to the social or moral aspects of management action.

A *political* orientation developed with the 1932 "New Deal" of President Roosevelt. Following World War II, government regulation reached an all-time high, while increased education and developments in the field of communication brought about a change in the structure of North American society. The threat and the reality of government regulation tended to be the primary force moving business to higher ethical standards. Thus businesses gained a political orientation toward ethical problems. The theory was that if business didn't meet its responsibilities the government would see to it that it did.

A *social system* orientation is now beginning to unfold. Marketing and other functional decision-making processes are being fundamentally altered as ethical considerations are being integrated into all business decisions through a total systems approach. The orientation goes beyond service and the profit motive toward accepting an obligation to help in the solution of major social problems. Moreover, emphasis is being placed on initiating solutions to these problems rather than merely responding to demands. This is a stage where management, with its broad responsibilities to society, will review all policies directly affecting the public interest—e.g., employment practice; product attributes, including quality and safety; advertising policies; and environmental issues—to consider their societal impact. It is in this stage that managers realize that the destiny of each corporation is inevitably tied to the destiny of society.

INTERNATIONALIZATION

The marketing executive also finds he is no longer confined to national boundaries. His role is changing from a national to an international businessman facing vigorous international competition. The internationalization of business presents new and perplexing problems and requires different strategies to achieve objectives.

The expansion of the American businessman to an international businessman is shown by J. J. Servan-Schreiber in *The American Challenge*. Servan-Schreiber states that the real strength of American industry in Europe is not based on technological superiority or abundance of resources (although these still remain important factors), but on flexibility and management skill.[7] The use of the marketing concept is a prime factor of this flexibility and skill. Servan-Schreiber quotes the following statement from an American executive in Frankfurt.

> If a German executive wants to increase his production, he studies all the factors that go into the manufacture of his product. But if I want to increase my production, I add to these same calculations our research and market predictions so that I will know not only how to produce, but how to produce the desired quantity at the lowest cost. What interests me is my profit margin. What interests my European competitor is a factory that produces. *It isn't the same thing.*[8]

This challenge of American businessmen to European businessmen is not being left unanswered.

> The performance of European Economic Community countries in world markets is, of course, a reflection of their success at home. From the consumer viewpoint, this is evidenced in what Americans are advised to take with them when they move to Europe; 10–15 years ago, the recommended "kit" included at least the major appliances, a full medicine chest, baby clothes for the first year and maybe a car.
> Now the picture has completely changed; while differences of style and performance persist, there are few goods available to the American consumer that are not produced at competitive prices in Europe, and one's counsel to the expatriate is to take little with him.[9]

Another significant indication of the international need for a marketing concept, whether in a capitalistic or non-capitalistic country, is illustrated in a Joint Economic Committee report on Soviet economic performance.[10] As a result of problems in previous five-year plans, the Soviet pattern of managerial incentives underwent a change noted by the Committee. Soviet managers were instructed to use such criteria as volume of sales, profit, and rate of return on capital for the decision-making process. At the same time, new emphasis was given to increasing the supply of consumer goods and increasing money incomes for the population. From these changes can be drawn the conclusion that this new economic growth program has at its base the profit concept and consumer emphasis. The Soviets are, in fact, attempting to use the marketing concept as a means of achieving continued economic growth.

[7] J. J. Servan-Schreiber, *The American Challenge,* trans. Ronald Steel (New York: Avon Books, 1969), p. 39.

[8] *Ibid.*

[9] John B. Rhodes, " 'The American Challenge' Challenged." *Harvard Business Review,* xlvii, No. 5 (September-October 1969), 45.

[10] *Soviet Economic Performance: 1960–67,* prepared for the Joint Economic Committee (Washington, D.C.: U.S. Government Printing Office, 1968), pp. 1–10.

Marketing as a Discipline

In its development as a discipline and area of study marketing has undergone many changes. Several approaches to marketing have developed over time—the classic institutional, functional and commodity approaches; the scientific-technological approach; the managerial approach; and social approaches have offered broader perspectives and new insights. Both the systems and the metamarketing approaches are utilized in this book, where they serve as a broader framework for examining the managerial approach.

Each approach to the study of marketing has utility and limits. Each is used to accomplish different objectives and for analysis of different kinds of marketing activities. Differences in corporate organization, industry, characteristics, background, and experience of marketing men also influence the approach used, as do the operational and organizational sequences required by different marketing problems. The major approaches to the study of marketing activities are summarized below.

Classical. The classical approach features consideration of the functions involved in transferring title to goods, the institutions (middlemen and facilitative agencies) that perform marketing functions, and the analysis of distribution on a commodity basis.

Scientific-Technological. This approach is reflected in decision theory and in various mathematical schools. It involves either (a) analysis and expression of management problems and decisions as mathematical relationships and models; or (b) analysis of, and emphasis on, the decision itself, those making the decision, or the decision process.

Managerial. The managerial approach emphasizes functions performed by marketing managers (assessment, planning, organization and leadership, evaluation, and adjustment). It involves the development of principles—i.e., fundamental truths or generalizations that aid in understanding and improving management in marketing—and the creation of theories based on these principles, along with business experience, micro-oriented toward profits, sales, and cost reductions.

Social. The social approach is based on the social sciences, history, and social philosophy. Three subtypes of this approach are the people-centered approach of psychologists, the social-systems approach of sociologists, and the approach of the marketing historian. Emphasis is placed on the desires and actions of individually unique, creative human beings, and on acts of intuition, volition, and purposeful will, which are then translated into practical courses of action, controlling what will happen. In general, the social responsibility orientation examines society as a whole and its interaction with marketing strategy.

The classical approaches are concerned with studies involving marketing institutions, functions, and products. These more traditional approaches have limits in their scope, but they present the foundations of the knowledge that the marketing executive must have. However, marketing has broadened its horizons and is looking beyond the firm and its immediate relations with buyers and suppliers, as is evidenced by the managerial and social approaches. In the managerial approach marketers look beyond the firm's internal environment toward external factors which affect it. This requires an examination of both the internal and external environments in an attempt to arrive at fundamental generalizations concerning the opportunities inherent in the market that can be actualized by proper planning of product, price, promotion, and distribution.

The social approach combines with the managerial approach in a search for an understanding of the consumer and the environment. It carries the study of marketing further into the frequently overlooked area of social responsibility. The growth of the scientific-technological approach reflects further changes in marketing and its study. Computers, research breakthroughs, and appropriate managerial adaptations suggest that a firm's use of an expanded viewpoint involving such factors as the internal and external environments and consumer attitudes may lead to greater customer service capability and greater growth potential.

The Systems Approach

An overview of the systems approach to marketing action defines the executive, not just as an executive of a firm, but as a businessman operating in a complex system of interacting variables, including all elements of the enterprise and the society in which he functions. Because the business environment is more complex today, a method is needed to give order to the many dynamic elements which must be considered by the executive. These include the day-to-day complications of corporate management as well as increasing societal pressures. The systems approach views a business enterprise as a total integrated system of business operating in a dynamic environment. The firm is not considered as a number of separate organizational units, processes, and activities. Therefore, the major task of marketing leadership is that of integrating all elements of the business into an effective system that will accomplish marketing objectives and the corporate mission to the mutual benefit of the firm and society. Most important, the systems approach to marketing always sees the attitudes and desires of the customer as paramount. This subject will be treated in more detail in Chapter 2.

Marketing's Broader Dimensions

While the emphasis of this book is on business management, marketing as a process is not strictly a business activity, nor is it possible to define marketing narrowly in terms of corporate activity. Marketing executives and students are now exploring new areas of inquiry and searching for new interrelationships to combine with the traditional conception of marketing. This exploration involves many fields directly and indirectly related to marketing. Because modern marketing management begins with analysis of environmental forces, needs, and opportunities, modern marketing goes beyond the management of products, prices, distribution, and promotion. Fundamentally, marketing involves assessing environmental change and new opportunities, planning to capitalize on opportunity, and structuring and managing resources to meet opportunities for service, growth, and profits both in established and in new operations.

Metamarketing: A New Approach

The diversity of approaches to the study of marketing reflects the varying interests and perspectives of marketing managers, management scientists, public policy makers, and consumers. Historically, marketing was viewed simply as the business of buying and selling; the concern with the institutions of marketing and the physical movement of goods followed naturally. The philosophy of marketing was relatively narrow and the objective was to achieve distribution of a product to the consumer with primary emphasis on the product and the selling firm. Over time, the study of marketing has been extended from a micro-oriented to a macro-oriented viewpoint. No longer is the product the primary focal point of marketing. Rather, marketing now concerns itself with such factors as the customer and his wants and needs, over-all functional interrelationships between what used to be defined as the province of marketing and other disciplines (as well as other parts of the business administration discipline), a societal perspective in the implementation of marketing, and a new technology in the tools of decision making.

The integration of the approaches to business problem solving is one of marketing's greatest challenges, and one that still another approach—metamarketing—attempts to meet.[11] The term *metamarketing*, in which *meta* is used as in metaphysics or metapsychology, to mean beyond, designates a new approach that deals critically with marketing as a field of study. Marketing offers multiple opportunities for speculation on the theoretical interrelationships between mental and physical processes and the facts, empirical observations, and experiences of marketing practice. The concern of metamarketing is to focus all scientific, social, ethical, and managerial experience on marketing in such a way as to build a marketing foundation based on a broad plan of experience, implemented by the systems approach, and taking into account the human personality.[12]

Metamarketing, which must be considered as an approach to the study of marketing activities, is currently in the domain of the marketing philosopher, as is outlined below.

[11] Eugene J. Kelley, "Ethics and Science in Marketing," in *Marketing Science,* ed. George Schwartz (New York: John Wiley & Sons, Inc., 1965), pp. 465–83. See also Eugene J. Kelley, "Ethical Considerations for a Scientifically Oriented Marketing Management," in *Science in Marketing Management,* ed. M. S. Moyer (Toronto: Bureau of Research, Faculty of Administrative Studies, York University, 1969), pp. 69–87.

[12] For a discussion of metaplanning, see Francis X. Kane, "Security is Too Important to be Left to Computers," *Fortune,* lxix, No. 4 (1964), 147.

Metamarketing. At present, metamarketing is essentially a speculative approach that deals critically with marketing as a discipline and with the application of quantitative, behavioral, and social concepts, models, and techniques to marketing problems in business and non-business areas. It attempts to accomplish a synthesis of the managerial, traditional, scientific, social, and historical foundations of marketing. With its speculations on the interrelationships of mental and physical processes to supplement the facts and empirical observations of marketing practice, metamarketing is an application of the whole of scientific, social, ethical, and managerial experience to marketing.

Business Orientation. The metamarketing concept has two main operational elements. The first, emphasized in this volume, is metamarketing as a business-oriented management field. Managers analyze marketing problems utilizing metamarketing analysis, recognizing the multiple dimensions of marketing problems—technical, social, legal, and institutional. Such managers are not reluctant to come to grips with the philosophical aspects of marketing.

The second element of metamarketing deals with the expanding scope of marketing in non-business organizations. There is growing awareness that marketing-oriented activities are not necessarily confined to the world of business and that there is opportunity to apply marketing science to fields not previously considered.

Organizational Furthering. "Furthering," which is one type of metamarketing thought, is defined in this book as metamarketing analysis synthesizing other approaches into a workable system of relationships to attain the goals of the firm as well as society as a whole. Levy and Kotler describe this furthering concept which transcends traditional boundaries of marketing.[13] Inasmuch as the structuring of market interrelationships and objectives is achieved with the aid of the systems approach, then metamarketing is a systems related approach.

The following table summarizes certain of the relationships discussed so far.

Orientations to Business Problems	Basic Views of Marketing	Prime Levels of Approach
Legal ("Let the Buyer Beware")	Selling	Functional
Political ("The Customer is King")	Customer Satisfaction	Managerial
Social ("Marketing as a Social Process")	As a Business and Social Discipline	Corporate-Systems

[13] Sidney J. Levy and Philip Kotler, "Beyond Marketing: The Furthering Concept," *California Management Review,* xii, No. 2 (Winter 1969), 67–73.

The marketing executive finds himself operating in a complex and afflu-ent society—a consumption-oriented society. As a result of this complex new environment it has become increasingly necessary for the executive to plan his strategy carefully. To do this he must have an understanding of the system in which he operates. The marketing executive must have an awareness of the important elements of the system, and must be familiar with many areas of knowledge; he must have a method of transferring this knowledge into an operational corporate strategy and a set of plans that will achieve the mission, objectives, and goals of the company. To minimize uncertainty, he must be able to establish a system to implement the strategy plan in the most efficient manner possible. Currently, these relationships are described in a pattern of business operation known as the "marketing concept," which is described below. This book, and other volumes in the Foundations of Marketing Series, develop applications of the "marketing concept."

Effective Marketing Orientation— The Marketing Concept

The application of the marketing concept is characterized by the acceptance and use of the following elements:

1. The company accepts change as the prime characteristic of modern marketing and monitors the environments of the firm in a continuing effort to discover new areas of marketing op-portunity. This involves a systems orientation.
2. The company appreciates and understands the consumer-citizen's strategic position as a determinant of the firm's sur-vival and growth. The entire marketing system is designed to serve consumer-citizen needs in companies operating under the marketing concept.
3. It is assumed that marketing activity which serves consumer needs can be planned, and that corporate destinies can be shaped, to a large extent, by planned marketing management effort.
4. Short- and long-range planning of company activities on a continuing basis, and the development of consistent strategies and tactics resulting in an integrated system of marketing ac-tion, are seen as the key marketing management task.
5. Marketing and business research is utilized to arrive at more fact-founded decisions than could be made by intuitive ap-proaches. Research, including a system of commercial intelli-gence, is becoming indispensable in modern marketing plan-ning and action.
6. The significant role of marketing intelligence in establishing corporate goals and targets is recognized. Market potentials, rather than production resources, become guides to corporate marketing action.
7. Intra- and interdepartmental implications of marketing de-cisions and actions of various organizational units are recog-nized, and the integration of all marketing effort is sought.

8. Programmed process and product innovation, including the development of a climate that encourages innovation, is accepted as standard and necessary.
9. New product planning and development and their impact on company profits and posture are recognized and emphasized in corporate policy.
10. A marketing focus is adopted to coordinate company effort and establish corporate and departmental objectives consistent with the firm's profit, growth, and social objectives.
11. There is a continual reshaping of company products, services, and other activities to meet the demands and opportunities of the marketing place more effectively.
12. The company constantly defines and redefines these elements and interrelationships within its frame of reference in order to systematize the discovery and implementation of marketing opportunity.[14]

While profit and customer satisfaction continue to be strong foundations of the marketing concept, the executive is placing new emphasis on such elements as the environment and information technology.

It is easy to pay lip service to the elements mentioned in the preceding discussion; it is difficult to make them operational. Taken separately, each element of the marketing concept seems easy to understand. In fact, many marketing concepts seem deceptively simple. In practice, however, marketing is quite complex, owing to the interaction of people and programs, of tradition and change. Even today most marketing managers will agree that the "marketing concept" represents a goal rather than a description of current conditions. One reason for this is that it is difficult to predict and manage the interaction of the twelve elements on our list in a fluid and open society. The last element of the marketing concept gains importance in this respect as it affords a means of examining the complex variables of goals, environment, research, and the customer in a continuing and interrelated framework.

[14] See Eugene J. Kelley and William Lazer, *Managerial Marketing: Perspectives and Viewpoints,* 3rd ed. (Homewood, Ill.: Richard D. Irwin, Inc., 1967).

2

INFORMATION AND SYSTEMS
MANAGEMENT IN MARKETING

A major marketing management problem is to develop an integrated marketing program by coordinating all the resources required to fulfill targeted consumer needs. This calls for skill in developing external programs and strategy as well as in developing internal programs. In external programs, the emphasis is on the total system, and the firm's relationship with other elements in the system. Internal programs require coordination between marketing and other activities of the business and between the various marketing elements comprising the total mix. Both tasks require an understanding of systems analysis.

Frederick Kappel, formerly Chairman of the Board of American Telephone and Telegraph Company, stated that the task of integrating technical resources depends basically on systems analysis and thinking.[1] The telephone network is a system in which no single element is meaningful by itself. Only when all elements are conjoined and function well is the usefulness of each revealed and the system as a whole given meaning. What is true of the telephone network is true of any complex enterprise. In marketing, this places a substantial burden on the executive who must determine the objectives of the system he is managing. The manager must ask himself such complex questions as: what is the map of the system; what are its boundaries; what are the parameters? This type of thinking emphasizes application of the principles on which systems engineering is based.

The total systems approach refers to the operations of the entire enterprise. A systems view of General Motors would involve analysis of the parent company, its various manufacturing units, and its numerous line and staff divisions throughout the world. The systems view can also be extended to include the multiple interrelationships between General Motors and its suppliers and dealers. Automobile agencies are independently owned, but they are definitely a part of the General Motors marketing

[1] Frederick Kappel, "Business and Science," a speech before the 13th International Management Congress, New York City, September 16, 1963.

system. The systems view can be extended even further to include General Motors customers, the government, and consumer groups. Such a total systems view of our largest corporations is probably too complex to understand fully at this time. But for analytical purposes it is necessary to consider major systems and subsystems of this type, because the key to analysis is a study of interrelationships and information flow.

A system is composed of many subsystems. These subsystems are all inextricably interrelated and the functions of each are crucial to the functioning of the system as a whole. Thus, coordination of parts must be obtained in order for total goals and objectives to be achieved.

The concept of the system as sets of parts involves viewing components, whether internal or external, in terms of inputs and outputs. Manpower, knowledge, promotion, channel management, products, and prices can be viewed as one set of inputs; competitive pressures as another; government and economic trends as a third; and customer and societal needs as a fourth. The accomplishment of the marketing goals of customer service and satisfaction, profit, growth, and socially responsible business practices can be viewed as outputs. Relationships must be developed to show the manner in which inputs and outputs interact with each other.

A system is defined operationally in terms of the dominant activity being described; for example, a manager can analyze a business system, a marketing system, or a physical distribution system. The emphasis in systems analysis is on the interrelations and interconnections of the elements. The systems approach to marketing influences a firm's basic thinking about its marketing organization. Envisioning its marketing organization as a goal-directed system can stimulate fundamental thinking about the firm's marketing operations and problems and its current and future selling tasks. A major contribution of the systems approach to marketing is that it requires the clear statement of precise goals toward which the system is aiming and encourages a logical and systematic process of analyzing the impact of marketing decisions.

Marketing systems, therefore, include the following components:

1. A set of functionally interdependent marketing subsystems, including people and institutions—e.g., manufacturers, wholesalers, retailers, facilitating agencies, and consumers.
2. Interaction between individuals and firms to maintain relationships and facilitate adjustment to change, innovation, cooperation, and competition.
3. Establishment of objectives, goals, targets, beliefs, symbols, and sentiments that evolve from and reinforce the interaction, thus producing realistic marketing objectives and programs, and creating favorable images, attitudes, and opinions.
4. A consumer-oriented environment within which interactions take place subject to the constraints of a competitive market economy, of the legal and socioeconomic environment, and of the evolving relationships and methods of marketing entities.
5. A technology of marketing, including communications media,

information technology, credit facilities, standardization and grading, marketing research, and physical distribution.[2]

Marketing and Change

A business operates in a number of environmental systems, including the industry itself, the community, the national and international scenes, and the technological and market systems. Each system represents opportunities, or threats, and has constraints requiring analysis by marketing men. Change in any of these external systems influences the firm and the firm's ability to utilize resources and capabilities to best advantage. Change is the prime characteristic of these environmental systems; the pressures of change on a global scale dominate marketing analysis and decision-making today. A major task of management is to match up developments in the external environment with the capabilities and resources of the firm.

An example of the rapidity of change is provided by Alvin Toffler.[3] Toffler describes the present period as the "800th lifetime." An estimated 800 lifetimes of approximately sixty-two years each have transpired during the past 50,000 years of man's existence on the planet Earth. When this period of prehistory and history is broken down into lifetimes, the present, or 801st lifetime, demonstrates an almost startling technological acceleration. As Toffler indicates, fully 650 of the first 800 lifetimes were spent in caves. Only during the last six lifetimes did the masses communicate by the printed word, only in the last two have they known the electrical motor, and the overwhelming majority of goods we use today were not developed until the present, the 800th lifetime, of which marketing itself is a product.[4] Formal university courses in marketing have been offered for only about sixty years.

According to Toffler and other futurists, the technologically advanced countries are at the brink of a new "super-industrial revolution" which will lead into "an entirely new plateau of civilization." It has been observed that the United States is at a new stage of social development and that world society is in an important transition era. As the agrarian age in the United States yielded to industrialization, so is the industrial age now undergoing a transition into a new era. Brzezinski describes this new era as the "technetronic era."[5] This term indicates the principle impulses of contemporary change—technolology and electronics. Though the validity of this view can be debated, its importance is that it illustrates the view of many that global society is in the midst of a major transition period. Mar-

---

[2] Eugene J. Kelley and William Lazer, *Managerial Marketing: Perspectives and Viewpoints,* 3rd ed. (Homewood, Ill.: Richard D. Irwin, Inc., 1967), p. 20.

[3] Alvin Toffler, *Future Shock* (New York: Random House, 1970), p. 15.

[4] *Ibid.,* p. 15.

[5] Zbigniew Brzezinski, *Between Two Ages* (New York: Viking Press, 1970), p. 14. See also Charles A. Reich, *The Greening cf America* (New York: Random House, Inc., 1971).

keters, among others, must study the change from several perspectives to identify new opportunities.

A marketing manager, like other managers, manages manpower, money, equipment, facilities, or in economic terms, the scarce resources of land, labor, and capital, to achieve corporate objectives. In this chapter the focus is on the management of change through the management of a critical resource-knowledge. The knowledge available to the firm provides the basis of the firm's distinctive competence in the market.

Knowledge is a factor of production. When combined with other resources it becomes the critical resource. The fact that the United States has spent more money on education than any other country is important in explaining our progress. The U.S. interest in education is also reflected in executive development programs designed to develop managerial talent.

The purpose of knowledge management is to plan for and develop programs which will capitalize on opportunities presented by change. Managers will increasingly be evaluated on the basis of their skills in combining personal and organizational knowledge with judgment to achieve solutions to business problems. This test of management skill will be superimposed on the assumption of technical competence in specialized business functions.

Businessmen are not concerned with the totality of knowledge in reaching decisions. In any given problem they are concerned with specific information to solve specific problems. The emphasis upon information, as opposed to general knowledge, underscores the applied nature of the business enterprise. The manager must evaluate new knowledge and organize it into informational form, from which the firm can design and implement plans to accomplish objectives. In contrast to the usual approach, which emphasizes each area separately, this emphasis is consistent with the meta-marketing approach which suggests a synthesis of the managerial, traditional, scientific, and social foundations of marketing. From these approaches, four basic knowledge areas, inherent in the five components of marketing systems, can be defined. They are: (1) Basic Marketing Knowledge, (2) Human Behavior, (3) The Environment, (4) The Decision Sciences.

Marketing in an Information Society

The importance of information management as a synthesizing and integrative management function means business is operating in what might be described as an *information society*. Not only is knowledge increasing more rapidly, but the facilities for producing information are also expanding. From an operational viewpoint, the concept of information management becomes critically important to marketing executives.

A key characteristic of the information society is a new information technology characterized by the computer and the powerful techniques of quantitative analysis. Computer developments such as real time, computer-graphics, time sharing, and library programs are matched with quantitative tools such as operations research, statistical techniques, and new methods of collecting and integrating information for problem solving and decision making. This new information technology is important in marketing problem solving for it affects not only the way in which we think about and formulate problems, but also the types of problems we choose to attempt to solve.

A corollary to the development of the information society is a new societal orientation to knowledge and information; which results in a new perspective for evaluating information, and particularly information supplied to consumers by marketing and advertising. The significance of societal changes can be observed in what is happening with youth, particularly the college age population. For the young, social forces are just as important as, or perhaps more important than, technological forces, in shaping new market demands and opportunities. As this group assumes more decision-making powers, new standards of marketing and advertising will develop. An example of the importance of the societal orientation is the ecology-pollution issue. The Boeing corporation's SST proposal was defeated in the United States Congress in 1971 on environmental grounds, in spite of the support of the President; it was defeated because of the viewpoint that the social costs of the noise and air pollution created would be greater than the economic benefits. If the SST had been ready in 1960 it probably would have passed the Congress. The environmental issue was not an important factor in business planning in 1960, but will be crucial during the 1970s.

Knowledge Areas
Underlying Marketing Decisions

The knowledge explosion and the emerging information society suggest a "future oriented" method for classifying knowledge and information for marketing. Marketing knowledge can be organized around knowledge areas, rather than around existing products, industries, organizations, or functions. While all of these are important in the long run, knowledge and its commercial development will determine additional classifications.

Managers must be anticipators of the future who consider the changing environment, the changing behavior of customers, the changing competitive forces, and the effects of these changes upon the present and future. They must be capable of utilizing tools available to them in order to meet the challenges of change. In short, if they are to compete successfully within the complex framework of a continuously changing business system, managers must be anticipators of change rather than mere reactors to it.

As noted earlier, four knowledge areas underlie the study and practice of marketing. While the emphasis must rest upon a synthesis of these areas, an overview of each individually serves to illustrate the complexity of the integrative task.

BASIC MARKETING KNOWLEDGE

Marketing thought has evolved from emphasis on a relatively descriptive set of principles to a complex set of operational concepts. The marketing executive cannot neglect the fundamental concepts of distribution, promotion, pricing, and product strategies. Much of the "bread and butter" of marketing is included in the classical functional, commodity, and institutional contexts.

For example, a marketing executive must have a knowledge of the industry and market structure within which he operates. He must understand the competitive structure of his industry, the existing and possible channels of distribution, and the nature of facilitating marketing institutions. The executive must also understand existing and possible institutional forms; he must be aware of the functions of marketing and the possibility of their use along the channel and with different institutional types; and he must have an awareness of different products and product types.

Dual Core Marketing Function. Two basic functions are performed on the basis of marketing knowledge. While they are elementary, they are often neglected by those companies which do not continually reassess their activities.[6]

The initial concern of the dual-core function is that marketing management should focus business effort on the customer's needs and desires, including those which the customer may not recognize. After identifying these needs, marketers can guide the firm in determining what should be provided as necessary products and services to satisfy customers. The second concern of the dual-core function is a more familiar one, namely, the need to persuade the prospective customer, through all the arts of selling and advertising, to purchase the products and services that have been developed.[7]

---

[6] See Fred J. Borch, "The Marketing Philosophy as a Way of Business Life," Marketing Series No. 99, American Management Association, 1957.

[7] For additional information on basic marketing knowledge see: Charles F. Phillips and Delbert J. Duncan, *Marketing: Principles and Practices*, 6th ed. (Homewood, Ill.: Richard D. Irwin, Inc., 1968); S. Watson Dunn, *Advertising: Its Role in Modern Marketing* (New York: Holt, Rinehart & Winston, Inc., 1969); William J. Stanton and Richard H. Buskirk, *Management of the Sales Force* (Homewood, Ill.: Richard D. Irwin, Inc., 1969); Philip Kotler, *Marketing Management: Analysis and Control*, 2nd ed. (Englewood Cliffs, N.J.: Prentice-Hall, Inc., 1971); John Fayerweather, *International Marketing* (Englewood Cliffs, N.J.: Prentice-Hall, Inc., 1970); E. Jerome McCarthy, *Basic Marketing: A Managerial Approach*, 4th ed. (Homewood, Ill.: Richard D. Irwin, Inc., 1971); P. D. Converse, H. W. Huegy and R. V. Mitchell, *Elements of Marketing* (Englewood Cliffs, N.J.: Prentice-Hall, Inc., 1952); Eugene J. Kelley and William Lazer, eds., *Managerial Marketing: Perspectives and Viewpoints* (Chicago, Ill.: Richard D. Irwin, Inc., 1967); John A. Howard, *Marketing Management: Analysis and Planning*, rev. ed. (Homewood, Ill.: Richard D. Irwin, Inc., 1963); Delbert J. Duncan and Charles F. Phillips, *Retailing: Principles and Practices* (Homewood, Ill.: Richard D. Irwin, Inc., 1959); Richard M. Hill, *Wholesaling Management* (Homewood, Ill.: Richard D. Irwin, Inc., 1963); Robert Bartels, *The Development of Marketing Thought* (Homewood, Ill.: Richard D. Irwin, 1962); D. Maynard Phelps and J. Howard Westing, *Marketing Manage-*

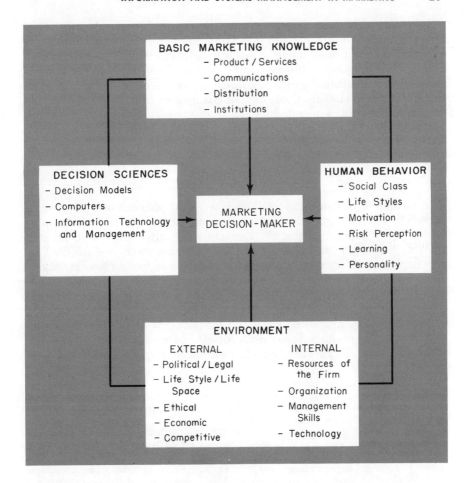

FIG. 2-1   Definable Knowledge Areas in Marketing

The Profit Concept. Modern marketing philosophy also rests, according to Borch, on the profit concept, not the volume concept. Volume is not eliminated as a rewarding way of obtaining profits; rather, Borch is referring to the profitless volume or volume-for-the-sake-of-volume concept.

ment, 6th ed. (Homewood, Ill.: Richard D. Irwin, Inc., 1963); J. D. Scott, *Advertising Principles and Problems* (Englewood Cliffs, N.J.: Prentice-Hall, Inc., 1953); David A. Revzan, *Wholesaling in Marketing Organization* (New York: John Wiley & Sons, Inc., 1961); Martin Zober, *Marketing Management* (New York: John Wiley & Sons, Inc., 1964); P. H. Nystron, ed., *Marketing Handbook* (New York: Ronald Press Company, 1948); T. N. Beckman, *Marketing,* 7th ed. (New York: Ronald Press Company, 1962); W. R. Davidson and P. L. Brown, *Retailing Management* (New York: Ronald Press Company, 1953); R. Barton, ed., *Advertising Handbook* (Englewood Cliffs, N.J.: Prentice-Hall, Inc., 1950); C. H. Sandage, *Advertising Theory and Practice,* 5th ed. (Homewood, Ill.: Richard D. Irwin, Inc., 1958).

Inherent within our economy are diverse technological and social changes, such as economic and population growth, as well as increasingly rigorous domestic and international competition, which have promoted changes in marketing institutions and processes. These include the appearance of new marketing forms, the breaking down of traditional product and institutional classifications, altered channels of distribution and organizational forms, an accelerated rate of product development and the application of new problem-solving tools to marketing problems.

HUMAN BEHAVIOR

The revolution of rising expectations is a global phenomenon. The world economy is becoming a consumption economy. In such a "Global Shopping Center" it is imperative that the marketing executive know who his customers are and that he be aware of their changing wants and needs. Factors important in customer decision-making include social class, life styles, risk perception, motivations, attitudes, learning, and personality differences.[8] These factors affect buying decisions and the customer's product adoption processes in complex ways.

Because every individual consumer has throughout his life been subjected to different stimuli and different environmental situations, no two individuals are exactly alike. People differ according to where they live,

[8] The marketer interested in a more detailed discussion of consumer behavior will find the following books useful: John A. Howard and Jagdish N. Sheth, *The Theory of Buyer Behavior* (New York: John Wiley and Sons, Inc., 1969); Harold H. Kassarjian and Thomas S. Robertson, eds., *Perspectives in Consumer Behavior* (Glenview, Ill.: Scott, Foresman & Company, 1968); Steuart H. Britt, ed., *Consumer Behavior and the Behavioral Sciences* (New York: John Wiley & Sons, Inc., 1967); M. Fishbein, ed., *Readings in Attitude Theory and Measurement* (New York: John Wiley & Sons, Inc., 1967); P. D. Martineau, *Motivation in Advertising* (New York: McGraw-Hill Book Company, 1950); Francesco M. Nicosia, *Consumer Decision Processes* (Englewood Cliffs, N.J.: Prentice-Hall, Inc., 1966); Gerald Zaltman, *Marketing: Contributions from the Behavioral Sciences* (New York: Harcourt, Brace and World, 1965); Carl I. Hovland and M. J. Rosenberg, eds., *Attitude Organization and Change* (New Haven: Yale University Press, 1960); James F. Engel, et al., *Consumer Behavior* (New York: Holt, Rinehart & Winston, Inc., 1968); G. H. Haines, *Consumer Behavior* (New York: The Free Press, 1969); George Katona, *Powerful Consumer* (New York: McGraw-Hill Book Company, 1960); Leon Levy, et al., *Consumer in the Marketplace* (New York: Pitman Publishing Corporation, 1969); Rom J. Markin, *Psychology of Consumer Behavior* (Englewood Cliffs, N.J.: Prentice-Hall, Inc., 1969); Chester R. Wasson and David H. McConaughy, *Buyer Behavior and Marketing Decisions* (New York: Appleton-Century-Crofts, Inc., 1968); John A. Howard, *Marketing; Executive and Buyer Behavior* (New York: Columbia University Press, 1963); Harper W. Boyd, Jr., and Sidney Levy, *Promotion: A Behavioral View* (Englewood Cliffs, N.J.: Prentice-Hall, Inc., 1967); J. H. Myers and W. H. Reynolds, *Consumer Behavior and Marketing Management* (Boston: Houghton Mifflin Company, 1967); Perry Bliss, *Marketing Management and the Behavioral Environment* (Englewood Cliffs, N.J.: Prentice-Hall, Inc., 1970); William Lazer and Eugene J. Kelley, *Interdisciplinary Contribution to Marketing Management* (East Lansing, Mich.: Michigan State University Press, 1959); Perry Bliss, ed., *Marketing and the Behavioral Sciences* (Boston: Allyn & Bacon, 1963).

the jobs they have, the social class to which they belong, the people with whom they associate, and in an infinite number of other ways. In short, no two customers have exactly the same wants and needs.

On the other hand, it is possible to identify trends and similarities in wants and needs and, consequently, in consumption patterns. Potential customers can be analyzed and distinguished by utilizing demographic and behavioral variables, and the total market can thus be segmented into several subgroups. The process of market segmentation is a basic activity.[9] Consumer panels, depth group and individual interviewing, mail surveys, and informal audits are important tools used by progressive marketers and many private researchers to understand and classify buyer behavior.

The question "Why do people buy?" has been studied by marketers for many years. One significant advance has been made by Howard and Sheth, who in their *Theory of Buyer Behavior* have integrated knowledge from psychology, sociology, anthropology, and the other behavioral sciences into a model of the buyer's decision-making process.[10]

One interesting manner in which the subject of human behavior may be approached is the examination of the life styles of consumers. Life style is an important concept for marketers because consumer life styles influence and shape economic activity. William Lazer defined life style as a systems concept:

> It refers to the distinctive or characteristic mode of living, in its aggregative and broadest sense, of a whole society or segment thereof. It is concerned with those unique ingredients or qualities which describe the style of life of some culture or group, and distinguish it from others. It embodies the patterns that develop and emerge from the dynamics of living in a society.
>
> Life style, therefore, is the result of such forces as culture, values, resources, symbols, license, and sanction. From one perspective, the aggregate of consumer purchases, and the manner in which they are consumed, reflect a society's life style.[11]

THE ENVIRONMENT

As previously noted, marketing executives must be environmentalists, anticipators of environmental change rather than mere reactors to it. This requires a knowledge of many factors affecting the firm both internally and externally. Within his own company, the marketing executive must

[9] For detailed discussion of market segmentation, see Wendell Smith, "Product Differentiation and Market Segmentation as Alternative Marketing Strategies," *Journal of Marketing* (July 1956), pp. 3–8.

[10] John A. Howard, and Jagdish N. Sheth, *The Theory of Buyer Behavior* (New York: John Wiley & Sons, Inc., 1969).

[11] William Lazer, "Life Style Concepts and Marketing," in *Toward Scientific Marketing*, Proceedings of the Winter Conference of the American Marketing Association, ed. Stephen A. Greyser (Chicago: American Marketing Association, 1964), p. 130. See also Eugene J. Kelley, pp. 164–71 in the same book.

have an understanding of such factors as the resources of the firm (financial, physical, human, and market), the organization itself, its management skills, and its technological capabilities. Of great consequence, also, are such characteristics of the external environment as the political, legal, sociological, ethical, economic, and competitive factors. Acquiring knowledge in these broad areas is a staggering task; however, such is the responsibility of the effective marketing manager.

An appreciation of the external forces that mold marketing opportunities and determine the profitability of the marketing effort of any firm is necessary for an understanding of modern marketing.[12]

American businesses operate in a market economy largely dominated by the actions of free consumers. But business and government are also dominating forces in American society. Actually, the actions of businesses, consumers, and government are interrelated. In a market economy, firms compete for the consumer dollar in a legal and ethical framework in which market action is molded by consumer activities and by both formal and informal market and social regulation. Existing legislation is one factor. The threat of further legislative regulation is another. More important, perhaps, are the forces that shape public opinion and the standards that grow out of consumer drives for personal and social well-being.

Marketing activities are inherent in the distribution of goods in all industrial societies, and marketing functions must be performed in any society where trade exists. In a controlled society the interests of the state, as defined by government policy-makers, dominate the production and distribution of goods. In a free society consumers ultimately determine what is produced and consumed, and the role of government becomes one of setting the legal boundaries and enforcing the rules of business conduct. These rules do much to mold the environment of business and the climate in which marketing decisions are made. In one sense, it can be said that the consumer finally controls the effectiveness of an individual firm's market policies; on a broader scale, it is the government, representing public consensus, which exercises the ultimate control over business. Although the role of government as a marketing regulator varies widely in international markets, marketing policy-making is influenced substantially by government policies and controls throughout the world. In some econo-

---

[12] Books and articles encompassing the environmental issue in marketing include: Lee E. Preston, ed., *Social Issues in Marketing* (Glenview, Ill.: Scott, Foresman & Company, 1968); Richard A. Scott and Norton E. Marks, eds., *Marketing and Its Environment: Some Issues and Perspectives* (Belmont, Cal.: Wadsworth Publishing Company, 1968); R. J. Lavidge and B. J. Holloway, *Marketing and Society: The Challenge* (Homewood, Ill.: Richard D. Irwin, Inc., 1969); J. H. Bearden, *Environment of Business: Perspectives and Viewpoints* (Holt, Rinehart, & Winston, Inc., 1969); R. J. Holloway and R. S. Hancock, *Environment of Marketing Behavior* (New York: John Wiley & Sons, 1969); William Lazer, "Marketing's Changing Social Relationships," *Journal of Marketing*, xxxiii, No. 1 (January 1969), 3–9; Phillip Kotler and Sidney J. Levy, "Broadening the Concept of Marketing," *Journal of Marketing*, xxxiii, No. 1 (January 1969), 10–15; Robert J. Lavidge, "Growing Responsibilities of Marketing," *Journal of Marketing*, xxxiv, No. 1 (January 1970), 25–28; Keith Davis, "Understanding the Social Responsibility Function," *Business Horizons*, x (Winter 1967), 45–48.

mies the government, rather than the market, provides the dominating marketing merchanism.

THE DECISION SCIENCES

One reason marketers are able to seek and reach new boundaries is that marketing operates in an age of technological and scientific advances. Currently available to marketing executives are high-speed computers, mathematical decision models, and quantitative tools that not only add to efficiency and precision but also provide capabilities never before accessible. Increasingly sophisticated models and tools are being regularly used by advanced marketing companies and marketing researchers. The computer has made possible new applications of Bayesian analysis, factor analysis, scaling techniques, queuing simulation models, multiple regression, cluster analysis, decision theory, discriminate analysis, and canonical analysis. As computer utilization becomes widespread, decision models and quantitative tools will be utilized more extensively.[13]

Through the use of better decision tools, marketers are able to undertake adventures once considered too risky. Thus, more efficient and sophisticated data manipulation permits a greater understanding of the customer, so that many of the uncertainties and risks of decisions are eliminated. In this sense, it is now possible for marketers to assume more risks and therefore contribute more to technological innovation.

The interchange of marketing and technological innovation is growing more significant. Recent economic thought has placed a higher assessment on the importance of expanding markets in creating conditions that lead to technical progress. After a study of more than nine hundred important inventions developed since 1900, it was concluded that in most cases the market was the mother of inventions, rather than the invention's being the mother of markets.[14] These findings imply that the basic impulse behind inventive genius may be the quest for profit. Of course, there are other incentives to invention, but profit-making through meeting market needs is basic.

More recent evidence proves conclusively that new technologies offer a prime source of economic growth. Many industries now earn most of their profits from products that did not exist twenty years ago. In the food industry, 62 percent of all products now available to the housewife were nonexistent ten years ago. More than five thousand companies engaged in

---

[13] Marketing aspects of the subject of decision sciences are discussed in: Ronald E. Frank, Alfred A. Kuehn, and William F. Massy, *Quantitative Techniques in Marketing* (Homewood, Ill.: Richard D.. Irwin, Inc., 1962); Frank M. Bass, ed., *Mathematical Models and Methods in Marketing* (Homewood, Ill.: Richard D. Irwin, Inc., 1961); P. Langhoff, ed., *Models, Measurement, and Marketing* (Englewood Cliffs, N.J.: Prentice-Hall, Inc., 1963); David B. Montgomery and Glen L. Urban, *Management Science in Marketing* (Englewood Cliffs, N.J.: Prentice-Hall, Inc., 1969); David A. Aaker, "Using Buyer Behavior Models to Improve Marketing Decisions," *Journal of Marketing*, xxxix, No. 3 (July 1970), 51–57.

[14] *Business Week* (May 16, 1964), p. 132.

missile-aerospace research and production have produced more than three thousand new products and techniques for use by private enterprise. This rate of growth indicates that a basic problem is to bring the powerful forces of science and technology to bear on serving the needs of the nation and the world.

Information Technology. Marketing's information technology rests on the systems view of marketing and business planning.[15] The management of information is shaping new dimensions in business planning by allowing managers to select, shift, screen, synthesize, and combine internal and external information inputs, in order to recognize the firm's relation to its customers, its competition and its environment in general.

Effective planning is becoming increasingly dependent on new ways of managing information, on more rapid and accurate identification of new markets, ventures, and products, and on closing the gap between business practice and advances in information processing technology. The ability to handle information effectively is an important component in a firm's profitability and even its survival. An increase in information flows has resulted in a situation where line managers find they must become good business planners. Planning is so dynamic that it is no longer acceptable to lean solely on staff to outline plans. Planning concepts should be internalized within the corporate structure so that it is as much a function of line management as possible, with staff personnel supporting and enhancing but not dominating the planning process.

[15] The following list of books and articles is provided for readers who wish to gain a deeper insight into the subject of marketing information systems: Richard C. Christian, "The Computer and the Marketing Man," *Journal of Marketing*, xxvi, 3 (July 1962), 79–82; Claude McMillan and R. F. Gonzales, *Systems Analysis: A Computer Approach to Decision Models* (Homewood, Ill.: Richard D. Irwin, Inc., 1965); Wroe Alderson and S. J. Shapiro, eds., *Marketing and the Computer* (Englewood Cliffs, N.J.: Prentice-Hall, Inc., 1963); Allan Fletcher, "Computer Science for Marketing Management—An Introduction to Opportunities and Techniques of EDP" (New York: New York Brandon Systems, 1967); I. S. Hugo, *Marketing and the Computer* (London: Pergamion, 1967); Richard H. Brien and James F. Stafford, "Marketing Information Systems: A New Dimension for Marketing Research," *Journal of Marketing*, xxxii, No. 3 (July 1968), 19–23; William F. Massy, "Information and the Marketing Manager: A Systems Analysis," *Computer Operations*, ii, No. 4 (October 1968), 7–18; P. E. Green, et al., *Experiences on the Value of Information in Simulated Marketing Environments* (Boston: Allyn & Bacon, Inc., 1967); Robert E. Malcom, *Computers in Business: A Fortran Introduction* (Scranton, Pa.: International Textbook Company, 1968); Charles P. Bonini, *Simulation of Information and Decision Systems in the Firm* (Chicago: Markham Publishing Company, 1967); D. F. Cox and R. E. Good, "How to Build a Marketing Information System," *Harvard Business Review*, xlv, No. 3 (May–June 1967), 145–54; Kenneth P. Uhl and Bertram Schoner, *Marketing Research: Information Systems and Decision Making* (New York: John Wiley & Sons, Inc., 1969); R. Ackoff, "Management Misinformation Systems," *Management Science*, xiv, No. 4 (December 1967); Samuel Van Dyke Smith, *Readings in Marketing Information Systems, A New Era in Marketing Research* (Boston: Houghton Mifflin Company, 1968); Arthur B. Toan, *Using Information to Manage* (New York: The Ronald Press Company, 1968); C. C. Barnett, Jr., and associates, *The Future of the Computer Utility* (New York: American Management Association, 1967); Philip Kotler, "The Future of the Computer in Marketing," *Journal of Marketing*, xxxiv, No. 1 (January 1970), 4–14.

These changes in information management indicate that marketing will be even more important in corporate planning during the seventies than it was in the sixties. *More businesses are redefining their goals, moving beyond the marketing concept to a view of the firm as an integrated technological and marketing system focusing on the profitable satisfaction of consumption needs.*

Underlying the new marketing technology is a conception of information which, until recently, was neither recognized nor appreciated by corporate planners. Today, more firms recognize that short and long-range operations cannot be properly conducted without proper information. They are also beginning to realize that if information is to be of value to the firm it must be utilized within the dimensional restraints of timeliness and executive time.

The recognition of the value of timely information as a resource accounts for the focus of the new technology. Information available for planning must be applicable to the time frame of the decision process if maximum benefit is to be obtained from it. In addition, it must be relevant to the problem area.

To insure availability of the appropriate information when needed, the marketing planner should ask the following questions in developing the information collection system:

1. What types of decisions are you regularly called upon to make?
2. What types of information do you need to make these decisions?
3. What types of information do you regularly get?
4. What types of special studies do you periodically request?
5. What types of information would you like to get which you are not now getting?
6. What information would you want daily? weekly? monthly? yearly?
7. What magazines and trade reports would you like to see routed to you on a regular basis?
8. What specific topics would you like to be kept informed on? [16]

The time dimension of information also plays an important role here. While technology can supply information faster than it could be supplied in the past, the critical demands rest upon the executive's time. In many situations the cost factor is overshadowed by the executive's time constraint. The effective executive, therefore, must deal with his time and available information as scarce resources within the affluent information society. It can be assumed that the return for the efficient use of these resources will be more effective communication and a more knowledgeable role in corporate decisions.

Incorporation of an information system designed to utilize the executive's time effectively will be a function of the planner's ability in answering the following additional questions:

[16] Adapted from Philip Kotler, "A Design for the Firm's Marketing Nerve Center," *Business Horizons* (Fall, 1966), p. 70.

1. What information should we collect?
2. How should we go about collecting this information?
3. How can we store the data so it is readily retrievable?
4. How can we best analyze it?
5. And how can we go beyond it through interpretations to get new ideas? [17]

Advances in marketing planning through information systems have been made possible largely as a result of an increased understanding of computer techniques and their application in areas of business interaction. Marketing information systems are the integration of data processing and communication capabilities. A marketing information system can be described as "a structured, interacting complex of persons, machines, and procedures designed to generate an orderly flow of pertinent information, collected from both intra- and extra firm sources for use as the bases for decision making in specified responsibility areas of marketing management.[18]

While such systems can be operational within the small firm without the use of a computer, they are next to impossible for the larger firm unless computer applications are understood and implemented at each management level.

It is the utilization of the computer for *information retrieval* and *computation* that allows planners to use meaningful information needed as inputs for complex decision tools, such as Bayesian analysis, scaling techniques, PERT and so on.

The computer's importance for planning cannot be overemphasized. However, there are many problems in integrating the computer into planning systems:

> . . . Computers are big, expensive, fast, dumb adding-machine—
> typewriters. . . . Most of the computer technicians that you're
> likely to meet or hire are complicators, not simplifiers. They're
> trying to make it look tough. Not easy. They're building
> a mystique, a priesthood, their own mumbo-jumbo ritual
> to keep you from knowing what they—and you—are doing.[19]

The following rule of thumb, adapted from Robert Townsend, is a guide for the adaptation and utilization of computers within the over-all corporate information system:

> At this state of the art, keep decisions on computers at the
> highest level. Make sure the climate is ruthlessly hard-nosed about

[17] John Howard, "Marketing's 'New Technology'" *Sales Management*, ciii, No. 10 (November 1, 1969), 23–25.

[18] Samuel V. Smith, Richard H. Brien, and James E. Stafford, "Marketing Information Systems: An Introductory Overview," in their *Readings in Marketing Information Systems* (Boston: Houghton Mifflin Company, 1968), p. 7.

[19] Robert Townsend, *Up the Organization* (New York: Alfred A. Knopf, Inc., 1970), p. 36.

the practicality of every system, every program, and every report. "What are you going to do with that report?" "What would you do if you didn't have it?" [20]

Marketers who follow these suggestions will find the computer system to be a valuable resource. They will have many more facts, estimates, and information inputs for their decisions. Philip Kotler has indicated several examples of the potentialities of the computer.[21] Each of the following programs is already available in one company or another.

> A new product manager can sit down at a terminal, dial a new product computer program called SPRINTER 1, and supply various estimates as they are called for by the computer, including the estimated size of the target group, recent product trial rates and repeat purchase rates, the promotional budget, size of investment, target rate of return, product price, and gross profit margin. The computer will digest this information and print out a monthly forecast for the next few years of the total number of buyers, company market share, period profits, and discounted cumulative profits. The new product manager can alter various input estimates and readily ascertain the effect of the altered data on sales and profits.[22]

> An advertising manager can dial a media selection computer program called MEDIAC, type in information on the size of his advertising budget, the number and size of important market segments, media exposure and cost data, ad size and color data, sales seasonality, and other information, and the computer will return a media schedule that is calculated to achieve maximum exposure and sales impact in the customer segments.[23]

> A sales manager can dial a sales redistricting program, type in data on the work load and/or sales potential of various counties, their distances from each other, and the number of sales territories he wants to create. The computer will digest this information and assign various counties to make up new sales territories in such a way that (a) the sales territories are approximately equal in work load and/or sales potential and (b) they are compact in shape, thus cutting down travel costs.[24]

---

[20] *Ibid.*

[21] Philip Kotler, "The Future of the Computer in Marketing," *Journal of Marketing*, xxxiv, No. 1 (January 1970), 11–14.

[22] Glen L. Urban, "SPRINTER Model: A Basic New Product Analysis Model," Alfred P. Sloan School of Management: Working Paper No. 397–69, Massachusetts Institute of Technology, 1969.

[23] See J. D. C. Little and L. M. Lodish, "A Media Planning Calculus," *Operations Research*, xvii (January–February 1969), 1–35.

[24] See Sidney W. Hess, "Realignment of Sales and Service Districts," Working Paper (Philadelphia, Pa.: Management Science Center, Wharton School, University of Pennsylvania, July 1968).

A marketing executive can dial a dealer site location program, type in a proposed location and size for a new dealership in a large city, and receive a forecast of sales and market share for the new dealership, and the loss of sales to other dealerships, including his own.[25]

A salesman can dial a sales prospect evaluation program, type in information about a list of prospects, including the estimated value of their annual business, the maximum probability of conversion, the estimated number of years they will remain customers, etc., and receive back a table suggesting the optimal number of calls to make on each prospect and how the prospects rank in order of attractiveness.[26]

The marketing controller can dial a dealer size evaluation program, type in data on annual sales of each dealer, servicing costs, and the behavior of unit production costs with scale of production. The computer program will suggest the minimum size dealer to retain.[27]

[25] T. E. Hlavac, Jr., and J. D. C. Little, "A Geographic Model of an Automobile Market," Alfred P. Sloan School of Management Working Paper No. 186–66 (Massachusetts Institute of Technology: 1966).

[26] Private program by Philip Kotler.

[27] *Ibid.*

3

MARKETING OPPORTUNITY ASSESSMENT

Entrepreneurial-Decision Functions

Knowledge of basic marketing principles, human behavior, decision sciences, and the environment is utilized in conjunction with information technology in the marketing mix and the over-all strategy plan through four entrepreneurial functions, which are (1) assessment of marketing opportunity, (2) planning and programming marketing effort, (3) organization and leadership of marketing activities, and (4) evaluation and adjustment of marketing effort.

ASSESSMENT OF MARKETING OPPORTUNITY

The function of assessing marketing opportunity involves identifying company goals and analyzing profit opportunities in order to determine the markets within which a company may try to achieve its objectives. Operationally, this function centers on the delineation of potential and actual customers. Continuous assessment assures that companies will be dynamic in their marketing and production operations, able to identify the challenges and problems facing them, and better prepared to meet changing market opportunities. The assessment function also stresses market opportunity as a key factor regulating company activity.

PLANNING AND PROGRAMMING MARKETING EFFORT

The over-all objective of marketing planning is to provide practical, fact-founded solutions for specific marketing problems. The analysis, synthesis, and interpretation of data gathered through marketing and business research are essential components of a marketing manager's responsibilities.

Obviously, planning is preliminary to, and cannot be separated from, the organizational, operational, and control aspects of business. To make planning central to the marketing concept in management, both short- and long-range planning are needed.

ORGANIZATION AND LEADERSHIP OF MARKETING ACTIVITIES

The rapid rate of new product development and the growing importance of international marketing are among the marketing changes that have raised organizational problems. The most dramatic organizational change has been the centralization of responsibility for the total marketing task under one executive who establishes, coordinates, and integrates all factors necessary to achieve marketing goals. This has resulted in upgrading the chief marketing executive to the level of vice president. At this level he can participate in all areas of business policy related to the marketing objectives of the firm.

EVALUATION AND ADJUSTMENT OF MARKETING EFFORT

The marketing manager uses various forms of controls to keep marketing efforts keyed to areas of profitable market opportunity. These controls include constant evaluation and adjustment. All methods have restrictive or restraining aspects, but they can also have motivational force. Controls include:

Management Controls. Control is based on clear-cut plans or stands, policies, and organizations established by management.

Financial and Cost Controls. Distribution cost accounting and control by function and product are standard forms of financial controls used in marketing. These types of control tend to be concerned primarily with expenses. The use of forecasts, quotas, and new technology characterizes both management and financial control.

Leadership Controls. Management and financial controls are integrated through personal leadership, working through the organization and motivation of individuals and groups. This is a more subtle type of control because it is concerned with the creative capabilities of people in an organization, and not just with the direction of motions or actions of groups of men. The objective of this type of control is to motivate the individual to achieve and exceed predetermined organizational and individual goals.

Integration Controls. This systems approach to control emphasizes the integration of all marketing activities. The marketing audit is a useful device to measure the extent of integration.

In this chapter we will discuss the first of these four entrepreneurial functions—the assessment of marketing opportunity. The remaining functions are discussed in subsequent chapters.

Assessment of Marketing Opportunity

The assessment of marketing opportunity is one of the most important challenges faced by marketing executives. Anticipated changes in the market environment must be analyzed and creatively related to the profitable use of corporate resources. Decisions reached from this assessment are then translated into marketing policies and plans. The policies and plans guide the company in its efforts to adapt to its economic and social setting and to achieve corporate goals.

The core of business policy requires top management to assemble the inputs which enable them to recognize present and potential customer wants. Management must also understand the effect of present strengths and limitations of the firm upon future production of want satisfying products for customers. Opportunity exists for the firm when resources are available to profitably satisfy present market demand or to cultivate and control future demand. The assessment of opportunity requires that knowledge resources become integrated by recognizing customer wants and evaluating the firm's ability to generate want satisfactions. The relationships between these activities are indicated in Fig. 3–1.

Prior to the 1960s management attention was focused on services and production rather than on customer want satisfaction derived from product and service benefits. Being product- and production-oriented instead of customer-oriented led to strategic errors in many large companies in several industries.

Theodore Levitt, in his statements concerning the railroad industry, vividly expressed the consequences of being product-minded without being customer-oriented.[1] The reason railroad growth stopped, in Levitt's view, was because railroaders failed to define their industry correctly. The railroads allowed or even encouraged other modes of transportation to take customers from them because railroad managements assumed they were in the railroad business rather than in the transportation business. Some leaders in the railroad industry, recognizing its "myopia," have attempted to change from a focus on trains and tracks to the focus of a service organization which provides economical transportation for the goods essential to the present American way of life. Whether or not the railroad industry as a whole will be able to overcome its limited perceptions remains to be seen. Levitt provides another example of this myopia in the motion picture industry which incorrectly defined its business as making movies rather than providing entertainment, and thereby failed for many years to develop appropriate policies reflecting the competition of television and changing consumer preferences.

As little as twenty-five years ago, business opportunity was limited more

[1] Theodore Levitt, "Marketing Myopia," *Harvard Business Review*, xxxviii, No. 4 (1960), 45–56.

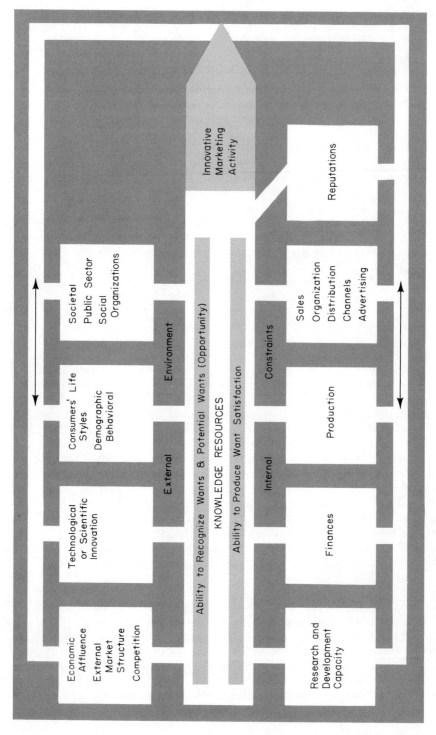

FIG. 3-1 Opportunity Assessment

by production capacity than by markets. In evaluating opportunity, managers were faced with less complex market structures and more unsatisfied, less complicated want structures on the part of customers. Firms were limited in their ability to produce such goods as transistors, color televisions, computers, and thousands of other products that were not yet conceived or were too expensive or complicated to produce. The 1970s should see major technological breakthroughs leading to new products and markets. For example, low cost mini-computers for the home are predicted at prices as low as $1,000. Navigational aids will provide safer air travel even in the presence of fog-shrouded airports, and plastic and paper will be used in making disposable linen-like fabrics.[2] "Ling-Temco-Vought plans to be ready with an automatic speed-monitoring computer that will sit discretely and unattended by the roadside, calculating the speed of passing cars; it will record the license—and photograph the driver—when cars break the speed limit. Selling for probably no more than $5,000 by 1975 it could be in use throughout the country."[3]

Two contrasting examples of marketing opportunity in today's environment serve to further illustrate the importance of a customer orientation in identifying opportunities. One large U.S. corporation learned that South American consumers wanted a simple but efficient clothes washing machine suited to their environment; this firm developed a hand-operated machine constructed to fit in a plastic pail which is successfully being sold for less than two dollars. The other example is the production of the Boeing 747 jumbo jet in response to the demands placed on the airlines by increasing passenger and freight loads. Each plane costs the airlines approximately $23 million and requires an additional three-quarters of a million dollars of ground service equipment. These costs do not include the millions that will be invested in new terminal facilities, personnel, and other required additions.

While production and product development played a necessary role in the satisfaction of both of these needs, an understanding of the customer and his environment played the leading role. The washing machine would never have been developed by the U.S. giant if the customer-oriented marketing concept had not been at work. Such an unsophisticated product would have been below the dignity of the advanced development and production capabilities of its Research and Development people. The jumbo jet would never have been constructed either, because without understanding customer wants the risk of investing the large sums of capital required for development and purchasing would have precluded construction.

In assessing marketing opportunity, the long-run view of resource adaptation recognizes that the most in ortant factor in capitalizing on marketing opportunity is not technological or financial, but conceptual. Informational resources of the firm must be used to identify and conceptualize

[2] C. G. Burck, "New Products of Tomorrow: A 1975 Sampler," *Fortune* (May 15, 1969), pp. 161, 218–32.

[3] *Ibid.*, pp. 226 and 232.

needs which can be satisfied, to create new demands, to find new markets, and to serve them profitably.

External Environments of Marketing

Environmental change is often the dominant factor in marketing decisions. For this reason marketing managers must be environmentalists. The rate and magnitude of change and its effect on the firm in the form of innovations, flow of new products, and competitive pressures are fundamental influences on marketing managers who are attempting to match customer needs and wants with corporate capabilities and resources.[4]

Correct assessment of marketing opportunity requires the identification and analysis of relevant factors in the total external environment surrounding the firm. One difficult conceptual task of management is to identify the specific external economic, technological, and societal factors relevant to the objectives and interests of the firm and to relate them to the resources of the firm and to the needs of customers.

External forces tend to set the direction and limits of market opportunity offered a firm and inevitably influence the firm's marketing strategy and organization. For example, product policies are determined by technological, cultural, social, economic, and even aesthetic considerations largely beyond the control of even the largest firm. This is true even though the largest firms, such as du Pont, American Telephone and Telegraph, and the like, may be active agents modifying the economic environment in which they function. One reason firms conduct public relations programs is that over time a firm can help to change the kinds of regulatory and competitive conditions it will meet in the future. Although a large firm can modify environmental conditions, it can rarely run counter to them. Even the largest firm is faced with a larger external constraining system that must be correctly analyzed.

Many forces are significant in the assessment of marketing opportunity and the determination of marketing policy. Some of the more important, identified in the first two chapters, include:

> An accelerating rate of technological change based on advances in knowledge in the sciences underlying industrial development.
> Changing life-style patterns and rising expectations of living standards on the part of consumers throughout the world.
> Continued development of the affluent society in the United States and the Western world and a drive toward economic development by other countries.
> Increasingly rigorous foreign and domestic competition in nearly all product areas.
> An increase in government influence and intervention and changing ideas about the nature of ethical issues in business.
> Changing concepts of marketing, communications, data processing, transportation, organization, and the styles of management.

[4] Eugene J. Kelley and William Lazer, *Managerial Marketing: Perspectives and Viewpoints,* 3rd ed. (Homewood, Ill.: Richard D. Irwin, Inc., 1967), p. 31.

Increasing concentration of power in fewer, larger companies, especially conglomerate enterprises.

Such forces necessitate management's concern for innovative competition. In this and the following chapter, the task of translating awareness of
environmental forces into programs designed to capitalize on opportunities
will be discussed.

External forces work as a constantly changing system in creating opportunities. At the same time, they reduce the attractiveness and future value
of opportunities previously actualized. An understanding of environmental
dynamics is a requisite to sound management of change, for opportunities
evolve from these interactions.

FUTURISM

Most business planning focuses on a one-to-five-year time span. The rate
of change indicated in this book, however, requires businesses to undertake some planning beyond this period. Such an expansion of planning
horizons directs efforts toward predicting the general shape of the future
in which the firm will be operating. In response to the need for such forecasting a field of futurism is developing, with its own literature and organizations. The development of a field of marketing futurism is certainly a
potential area of study which may grow in importance.[5]

Analysis of Environmental Forces

For purposes of marketing analysis and explanation, environmental
forces are classified as (1) economic and political, (2) technological and
scientific, (3) consumer, and (4) societal.

ECONOMIC AND POLITICAL FORCES

Affluence vs. Scarcity. The world market ranges across a spectrum from
relative scarcity and extreme poverty conditions in many industrially de-

[5] Some books written by futurists which are of interest to marketers include
the following: Alvin Toffler, *Future Shock* (New York: Random House, Inc., 1969);
Zbigniew Brzezinski, *Between Two Ages* (New York: Viking Press, Inc., 1970); Her-
man Kahn and Anthony J. Wiener, *The Year 2000: A Framework for Speculation*
(New York: The Macmillan Company, 1967); Harrison Brown, *et al., The Next
Hundred Years: Man's Natural and Technological Resources* (New York: Viking
Press, Inc., 1957); Burnam P. Beckwith, *The Next 500 Years* (Jericho, N.Y.: Exposi-
tion Press, Inc., 1968); John McHale, *The Future of the Future* (New York: George
Braziller, Inc., 1969); Dennis Gabor, *Inventing the Future* (New York: Alfred A.
Knopf, Inc., 1964); Gerald Feinberg, *The Prometheus Project* (Garden City, N.Y.:
Doubleday and Company, Inc., 1969); Daniel Bell, ed., *Toward the Year 2000:
Work in Progress* (Boston: Beacon Press, Inc., 1969); Donald Michael, *The Unpre-
pared Society: Planning for a Precarious Future* (New York: Basic Books, Inc.,
1968); Arthur Clarke, *Profiles of the Future* (New York: Harper and Row, Publish-
ers, Inc., 1963).

veloping countries to relative affluence in highly developed countries such as the United States and several western European countries. The rising aspirations of people throughout the world are catalyzed by the level of affluence reached in the United States, yet the means to the end of affluence are culturally relative. These means require close scrutiny by creative executives seeking marketing opportunity.

As countries develop economically, the nature of marketing opportunity changes. Economic development in the United States typifies this relationship. During times of relative scarcity, income and purchasing power were limited and staple goods (goods for the maintenance of life) consumed a large portion of that income. Marketing opportunity then existed in producing cheaply to satisfy this need for basic goods. As production increased, the supply of goods, money, and employment also increased, which permitted the purchase of more discretionary goods. The success of the Model T Ford is a good example of purchasing demand during earlier periods of American history. It was a simple, well built, no-nonsense auto. By contrasting the Model T to today's high performance, luxury automobiles that can be purchased with optional equipment equaling in value the cost of the basic automobile, it is easy to see the influence of affluence on our marketing structure.

> By the mid-1970's the U.S. will have a trillion dollar economy and a $3.9 trillion GNP by year 2000. . . . *Fifteen million new jobs in the U.S. will have to be created by 1975.*[6]

These statistics indicate that affluence will increase in our society. The distribution of that affluence will be an important variable for speculation and action. The individual, small enterprise, big business, and the state will all play important roles in this development. John Kenneth Galbraith has made several provocative observations concerning affluence in our society. He contends that big business is playing an increasingly dominant role in regulating our economy.[7] Its influence is felt by every individual in this country and by people in most parts of the world. Another author states that the third large power in the world, behind the U.S. and Russia, will be U.S. business in Europe.[8] This idea, combined with Galbraith's suggestion that U.S. giants could also conceivably hold the dominant power in this country, implies that the two greatest powers in the world may be Russia and U.S. business. Galbraith states, ". . . if economic goals are the only goals of the society it is natural that the industrial system should dominate the state and the state should serve its ends. If other goals are strongly asserted, the industrial system will fall into its place as a detached and autonomous arm of the state, but responsive to the larger purposes of

[6] Chamber of Commerce of the United States, *Washington Report*, viii, No. 34 (December 1, 1969), 2.

[7] John K. Galbraith, *The Affluent Society,* 2nd ed. (Boston: Houghton Mifflin Company, 1969).

[8] J. J. Servan-Schreiber, *The American Challenge,* trans. Ronald Steel (New York: Avon Books, 1969), p. 35.

the society." [9] It is to these larger purposes of society that marketing has the opportunity to make its most salient contribution.

External Marketing Structure. The external marketing structure is an important aspect in any economy. Institutional changes in the form of shopping centers, discount houses, service centers, credit card systems, and many other advances have created opportunities for progressive marketers. Independent merchants have been forced, by public demand for variety and convenience, to join hands with other retailers to provide the scope and style of shopping outlets that satisfy the wide and diverse range of buyers.

The increase in vertically integrated marketing systems, which Davidson classifies as corporate, contractual, and administered, has also been an influential force.[10] "Vertical marketing systems . . . consist of networks of horizontally coordinated and vertically aligned establishments which are managed as a system. Establishments at each level operate at an optimum scale so that marketing functions within the system are performed at the most advantageous level or position." [11] Chain stores that increasingly seek to control manufacturing facilities through ownership or long-term contractual arrangements are good examples of vertically integrated systems. Such structures offer economics of scale which often result in competitive advantages which independent operators find it hard to match. Companies are increasingly looking for ways to reduce uncertainties in the supply of salable goods and for ways to control the marketing of their manufactured goods at the retail level. The trend toward more vertical integration will be an important force throughout the seventies.

Institutional life cycles are accelerating in the same manner as product life cycles. As changes are introduced into distribution they are quickly absorbed. Marketers who lag in recognizing these changes soon find themselves far behind the innovators.

A greater variety of products is being offered in single retail outlets than ever before. This intertype competition results in "one-stop shopping" with mass merchandising the key to selling. Advertising becomes more important because salesmen tend to become decreasingly brand loyal, placing a greater emphasis on total volume sales.

J. C. Penney, Sears Roebuck Company, and several other organizations are developing into "free-form" corporations maintaining the flexibility to compete in several markets with varying retail structures. These organizations are willing to leave their traditional patterns and use their vast intellectual and financial resources to compete in such diverse ways as maintaining drugstores, mail-order houses, automotive service centers, insurance companies, and franchising organizations.

One notable development is the increased polarity of retail trade; that

---

[9] John K. Galbraith, *The New Industrial State* (Boston: Houghton Mifflin Company, 1967), p. 399.

[10] For discussion, see William R. Davidson, "Changes in Distribution Institutions," *Journal of Marketing,* xxxiv, No. 1 (January 1970), 7–10.

[11] *Ibid.,* p. 8.

is, there is greater concentration at the two extremes in retail outlets: the supermarket mass-merchandisers and the small specialty shops. Marketers are realizing that medium-size outlets handling a small variety of general goods do not offer the customer services necessary to compete with mass merchandising. Specialty stores provide the unique service and personal contact which yields one selling approach, while mass merchandising captures the convenience shopper.

Finally, customer desire for time and place utility will increase the use of vending machines, catalogue sales, and home sales techniques such as Avon uses.

Marketers should be ready to employ any or all of these changes to their benefit. Distribution practices in these forms are shaping many packaging, product development, and promotion policies.

Competition. The nature of competition is an important economic force to be integrated with opportunity assessment. The aggressive marketer understands that activities undertaken by his firm will encourage competitive reaction and that the nature of this reaction must be anticipated in assessing his own situation. At the same time activities initiated by other members of the economic community will create and limit the opportunities perceived by the marketing executive.

For example, in the early 1960s several U.S. chemical firms simultaneously recognized a gap in the European synthetic goods market.[12] Anxious to expand their markets, all leaped into the Common Market. Subsequently two large U.S. manufacturers, suffering from intense competition and acute cultural shock, were compelled to withdraw their operations at a loss of several million dollars. These losses might have been prevented, had the firms anticipated the competitive pressures they experienced.

Through an understanding of competitive influences on customer behavior, drug companies and many other firms have been able to advance their market shares in relatively fixed demand market segments. The market for antibiotics is an example. Although the market size is determined by the amount of illness requiring treatment, competition comes into the picture because four or five relatively distinct classes of drugs can be used by doctors to satisfy the need. New drug entities introduced into this segment come under competitive attack by strong marketers of the existing drugs. To overcome this pressure Bristol-Meyers, in its strategy for Polycillin (a brand of ampicillin—a new drug class), first established itself as the originator of the new drug and then licensed the product to other leading drug firms. The combined marketing efforts of several competitors established a high primary demand for the new drug class. Bristol-Meyers sales continued to rise because of the differential advantage of being first in the market with a drug entity sanctioned by several other well respected drug houses.

Another example illustrates how competitive activities can provide opportunities. Caterpillar Tractor has a policy of being second in the market

    [12] John Davenport, "The Chemical Industry Pushes into Hostile Country," *Fortune,* lxxix, No. 4 (April 1969), 108–15.

with the best. They are not primarily concerned with new equipment innovation; rather, they tend to allow the competition to introduce product advances. Yet this policy of following up successful competitive innovations has given them sales in excess of $1.7 billion, and leadership in the heavy equipment industry.

TECHNOLOGY AND SCIENTIFIC ENVIRONMENTAL FORCES

Technological advance is probably the greatest change agent affecting human life styles. Technology has changed at an exponential rate and has carried with it a change in human values. Research and technology create change by destroying old values and patterns of behavior. Technology also creates new opportunities. A technological breakthrough can make new life styles possible and can give individuals and society new options from which to choose. For example, the impact of the automobile, television, and computers on society goes far beyond technology and directly to social value changes. The creation and delivery of these new options by marketers are essential ingredients in business innovation.

Perhaps the most cogent example of technological impact on business is afforded by the computer. Computer marketing is, in a real sense, the marketing of a way of life to businesses. Moreover, the products of advanced technology require increased sophistication in the conceptualization of marketing opportunity. Thus the impact of technology combined with societal demands both enforces a creative approach to opportunity assessment and necessitates an integrative approach to structure the assessment process with regard to the combined impact of marketing outputs upon the consumer-citizen.

CONSUMER FORCES

In both domestic and international marketing, analysis of many marketing problems begins with consumers as the important focal point of all marketing action. The level of consumption in a culture is in a large measure determined by the character of that culture and the attitudes and behavior of consumers living in it.

Marketing approaches converge on the area of consumer behavior and any new knowledge about consumer attitudes, needs, and habits is important. Consumer behavior and business responses to this behavior are determined by multiple influences and in turn influence economic, political, societal, technological, and scientific dimensions.

Analysis of consumers can be divided into two interrelated phases: demographic analysis and behavioral analysis. The first deals mainly with quantitative elements such as age, sex, education, income, geographic concentrations and dispersions. The second describes more qualitative aspects such as personality, attitudes, risk perceptions, and motivations.

Demographic Factors. In using demographic analysis the decision-maker assumes that behavioral traits are relatively homogeneous among certain socioeconomic and geographical segments. The quantification of demographically describable aspects of the population can give the marketer an objective outline of the broader confines of the market. Most good demographic analyses combine several of the following factors.

POPULATION. Population increases and decreases are of prime interest to marketers.[13] For example, the possibility that the world population will reach seven trillion within the next thirty years, and that there will be 325 million Americans are basic facts which must be taken into account in long-range planning. To feed the world population in 2000 A.D., world food production will have to quadruple—a great opportunity for nutrition marketing. In this country, population increases may create a market for 200 million cars by the year 2000, three times the present total.[14]

INCOME. The center of economic power is shifting to the middle of the upper income group in the United States. Several million American families have annual incomes of more than $15,000. This group, which controls over a third of the country's buying power, largely determines the style of living of the middle class and therefore exerts a strong influence on what is marketed. The higher level of family income is frequently secured because a second wage-earner is employed. By 1975 there will be 33 million women working, 25 percent more than during the previous decade.[15] The combination of high incomes and working wives means that more dollars will be spent on convenience products, luxuries, and items that do not conform to the normally accepted definition of food, clothing, and other necessities.

LIFE CYCLE. A person's position in the life cycle is significant in influencing expenditures for many items. Life cycle analysis leads to clearer identification of such markets as the teen age, young adult, middle age, and old age markets. Further segmentation produces a male teen-age market and female teen-age market, and also identifies that portion of these markets which is college-oriented. Within the very near future, over half the U.S. population will be under age 26.[16] The changing life cycle of this youth market requires more subtle understanding.

Family life cycle, a quantitatively descriptive analysis of family units, is also important. The large numbers of newly married people, the practice of family planning through birth control, and the increased incomes of younger citizens are important changes in the market environment.

OCCUPATION—EDUCATION. Occupation may tell a great deal more about

---

[13] For a full discussion on this topic see Philip Kotler, *Marketing Management: Analysis, Planning and Control* (Englewood Cliffs, N.J.: Prentice-Hall, Inc., 1967).

[14] Chamber of Commerce of the United States, *Washington Report*, viii, No. 34 (December 1, 1969).

[15] *Ibid.*

[16] *Ibid.*

consumer behavior than income does. A carpenter or bricklayer may earn the same amount as a college professor or lawyer yet their interests and purchasing patterns may be considerably different.

The increase in the educational level of the population should also be noted. Not only is the amount of education increasing, but the quality is advancing. Computers are being used in grade schools to assist children under ten in studying foreign languages. Individuals reaching universities as freshmen now already possess greater knowledge in many respects than college graduates had fifteen years ago. Their view of the world is different and requires creative approaches which differ from those used with other market segments.

GEOGRAPHIC. Geographic segmentations can be made on a local, national, or international basis depending on market structure and corporate activities. Firms such as Singer, Caterpillar Tractor, and Unilever are viewing the whole free world as a market, without special focus on any one country. This wide geographical interest requires information systems extensive enough and flexible enough to measure diverse parameters. There are also important geographical considerations within this country. Long-term population shifts have reached the point where more people now live in suburban areas than in cities.[17] Moreover, the concept of megalopolis is coming closer to a reality,

Behavioral Factors. Newer marketing tools that foster a better understanding of consumer behavior have opened a new level of opportunity assessment. The marketing team that takes advantage of these new behavioral concepts may gain the competitive advantage necessary to become the marketing leaders in the years ahead. John Howard explained in simple terms the relationship between consumers' attitudes and motives and their behavior that provides the foundation for this new approach.

> Say a housewife has a preference for Brand A coffee. That's an attitude. You ask her to rate on a scale how she likes Brand A, and she'll do it. She can also tell you what dimensions, such as taste and strength, contribute to this preference. Now behind that attitude is a set of motives. If this lady has a stronger achievement motive than her neighbor, she may pay more attention to price. So the motives operate via attitudes. Right now we're working very well at the attitude level, and I'm optimistic that we'll make the connecting link between attitudes and the underlying motives.[18]

Personality variables are also being studied as a means of market segmentation. Philip Kotler lists seven such variables that may be determinants of buyer behavior:

---

[17] *1970 Census* (Preliminary).

[18] John Howard, "Marketing's New Technology," *Sales Management* (November 1, 1969), p. 24.

Compulsiveness	Compulsive; noncompulsive
Gregariousness	Extrovert; introvert
Autonomy	Dependent; independent
Conservatism	Conservative; liberal; radical
Authoritarianism	Authoritarian; democratic
Leadership	Leader; follower
Ambitiousness	High achiever; low achiever [19]

ATTITUDES. An understanding of consumer attitudes is basic to marketing planning and program development. Attitude change or stasis is one of the most important aspects of marketing strategy. Motivation, personality, and other psychosocial variables are increasingly being studied. Proper opportunity assessment requires that decision-makers understand the cause and effect relationship between possible company activities and consumer attitudes. These new marketing techniques are making such assessment possible. The blending of anticipated innovations with present and anticipated consumer attitudes and life styles is the foundation for successful marketing strategy in the world of change.

SOCIAL CLASS. Social class has been defined in terms of many different descriptive measures, among which income and occupation are the most commonly accepted. Recently, researchers have found that social class is defined by the individual's self-concept and not necessarily by income, education, or any other easily quantifiable variable. To understand social class and other behavioral traits, marketers have made giant strides in developing a behavioral approach to consumer opportunity assessment.

SOCIETAL FORCES

Marketers are becoming increasingly aware of the importance of societal factors in the assessment of marketing opportunity. Two separate but interrelated aspects comprise the social environment forces: (1) the growing public sector which operates as a unified consumer in social and environmental areas, and (2) social organizations providing societal want and need satisfactions to all consumers, recognizing the growing importance of ethnic and economic minority consumers.[20]

[19] Kotler, *Marketing Management*, p. 46.

[20] Since consumerism is becoming increasingly important to the marketing decision process, the reader desiring a broader understanding of this phenomenon, would be well advised to focus on the following readings: David A. Aaker and George S. Day, *Consumerism* (New York: The Free Press, 1971); Robert O. Herrmann, "Consumerism: Its Goals, Organizations and Future," *Journal of Marketing*, xxxiv, No. 4 (October 1970), pp. 55–60; Richard H. Buskirk and James T. Rothe, "Consumerism: An Interpretation," *Journal of Marketing*, xxxiv, No. 4 (October 1970), pp. 61–65; Raymond A. Bauer and Stephen A. Greyser, "The Dialogue That Never Happens," *Harvard Business Review*, xlvii, No. 1 (January–February 1969), pp. 122–28; Louis L. Stern, "Consumer Protection Via Increased Information," *Journal of Marketing*, xxxi (April 1967), pp. 48–52; Senator Warren Magnuson and Jean Carper, *The Dark Side of the Marketplace* (Englewood Cliffs, N.J.: Prentice-Hall,

The giant public sector of the economy accounted for $185 billion in expenditures in 1969. Over $80 billion of this went for defense. Indications are that in the 1970s more public funds will go to support such large business ventures as advanced transportation systems, antipollution investments, oceanographic exploration, and medical care.

"Consumerism," referenced in a recent article by Day and Aaker, as ". . . a *widening* range of activities of government, business, and independent organizations that are designed to protect individuals from practices (of both business and government) that infringe upon their rights as consumers . . ." has played an expanding role in the environment of business decision makers.[21]

Corporations are now beginning to feel acutely the social responsibility they have to all citizens in making many of their decisions. Never before have such large commitments in resources been made in carrying out corporate competitive strategy. The size of companies and lead time required for product development can result in significant societal impact. The jumbo jet is a good example of such an impact. Another good example is the millions of dollars drug manufacturers have committed to research on such entities as cancer drugs or mind enhancing chemicals. One drug house expended $8 million per year on inhouse research on mind drugs and to date has not reaped a single marketable product in the area. Once a drug entity is discovered, five years of testing and a Food and Drug Administration investigation will be required before the benefits will be felt by consumers.

A computer manufacturer developing a fourth-generation computer is producing not only a computer but an instrument of social change. The marketing opportunities for such advanced equipment are directly related to the abilities of people to use the equipment. Ultimately, use of such equipment will probably result in a whole new system of information distribution, with remote input/output terminals available to much of the population, and new concepts of computer utilization in business and other areas.

The second type of societal marketing opportunity involves organizations outside the traditional business sphere—organizations such as the United States post office, anti-cigarette groups, pollution control groups, or the American Medical Association.[22] "This poses . . . a great opportunity for marketing people to expand their thinking and to apply their skills to an increasingly interesting range of social activity. The challenge depends on

---

Inc., 1968); Vance Packard, *The Waste Makers* (New York: David McKay, 1960); Earl A. Clasen, "Marketing Ethics and the Consumer," *Harvard Business Review*, xlv, No. 1 (January–February 1967), p. 79; E. B. Weiss, *A Critique of Consumerism* (New York: Doyle, Dane and Bernbach, 1967); E. B. Weiss, "Marketers Fiddle While Consumers Burn," *Harvard Business Review*, xlvi, No. 4 (July–August 1968), p. 45.

21 George S. Day and David A. Aaker, "A Guide to Consumerism," *Journal of Marketing*, xxxiv, No. 3 (July 1970), 12.

22 *Business Week*, No. 2025 (June 22, 1968), p. 64.

the attention given to it; marketing will either take on a broader social meaning or remain a narrowly defined business activity." [23]

Opportunity Assessment

Theodore Levitt expressed a needed word of caution about opportunity assessment when he observed that,

> Modern soothsayers, by combining computers with crystal balls, can parlay old dogmas into modern disasters. . . . There can be a need, but no market; or a market but no customer. When Pittsburgh's steel mills shut out the sun at high noon 30 years ago, the need for pollution control was obvious. But there was no market then; nobody thought of doing anything about the smog, even though techniques for controlling it were available.[24]

To illustrate the problem of having a market but no customers, the example of a joint General Electric and Time, Inc. venture is cited. These two companies, recognizing the need for better educational materials, organized the General Learning Corporation in 1965. The combination of executive leadership from a newly resigned U.S. Commissioner of Education, electronic equipment from General Electric, and a huge library of educational materials from Time was visualized as the perfect combination to satisfy the market. The reason for the massive failures that resulted is not that the forecasters were wrong, but that the existence of a market does not assure the automatic existence of a customer. There are not customers large enough to buy the elaborate new educational technology visualized by the company founders; no school board could afford the capital outlays necessary. The product that is most sensible to produce is too costly to produce and therefore too costly to buy. With no customer large enough to buy it, the product does not get produced.

Marketers have long been concerned with assessing marketing opportunities. What is relatively new about the situation is that (1) opportunities are changing rapidly, and (2) a powerful information technology for problem-solving is developing in this area. Specifically, the combination of the computer and communications techniques is expanding management opportunities for problem-solving.

In addition, a combination of behavioral research and quantitative methodology has improved the quality of information and sharpened the focus

[23] Philip Kotler and Sidney J. Levy, "Broadening the Concept of Marketing," *Journal of Marketing*, xxxiii, No. 1 (January 1969), 10.

[24] Theodore Levitt, "The New Markets—Think Before You Leap," *Harvard Business Review*, xlvii, No. 3 (May–June 1969), 53–54.

on emerging opportunities. John Howard explained the underlying reasons for the advances that are being made in the area:

> First, there is the merger in psychology in which cognitive, learning and motivation theories have begun to come together. Second, two types of research in marketing that were largely separate in the period 1955 to 1965—the quantitative and behavioral approaches to buyer behavior—have since joined into a single stream.[25]

The use of computer technology to interrelate demographic and behavioral data should provide realistic aggregate customer profiles within the very near future. The quantification of qualitative behavioral models is possible only through the use of computer technology which allows for the thousands and even millions of variable combinations necessary for such an assessment.

Market Segmentation

Market segmentation involves dividing a large market—the total market for cars, clothes, computers, or any other product—into a number of smaller, more homogeneous markets. Segmentation can be demographic or behavioral. For example, the market for automobiles may be divided into the following segments, each of which may require a different marketing strategy to approach particular customer groups inasmuch as each variable may have a different effect on buyer behavior in a particular transaction.

Demographic	Behavioral
Age	Personality variables
Sex	Social class
Income	Attitudes
Education	Values
Occupation	Motives
Geographic locations	Culture

It is not a question of using either demographic or behavioral analysis. Full understanding of a market requires understanding of all of these bases of segmentation and their interaction. Both demographic and behavioral influences interact to determine market reaction to a new product or consumer reaction to an advertising campaign.

[25] John A. Howard, "Buyer Behavior and Related Technological Advances," *Journal of Marketing*, xxxiv, No. 1 (January 1970), 21.

Segmentation analysis produces stereotypes of markets which can be useful for certain product, promotion, and distribution purposes. It is never to be forgotten that each consumer is an individual with varying characteristics which must be taken into account by marketers and reflected in product plans offering a variety of individualized features. We will now examine one of these variables, age, in more detail by concentrating on one particular market segment—the youth market.

THE YOUTH MARKET

As indicated, age is one way to segment a market. A common age classification follows:

Age	
0–12	child
13–18	teen age
19–25	young adult
26–34	adult
35–49	middle age
50–64	old age
65 and over—senior citizen	

Each of these larger segments is still not defined precisely enough for marketing planning purposes. One attempt to break down the youth market, for example, produces the following segments indicating age, development, and educational level.

Age	Development	Educational Level
0– 5	baby	pre-school
6– 9	child	elementary school
10–14	pre-teen and teen	junior high school
15–18	adolescent	senior high school
19–22	young adult	college-undergraduate
22–25	young adult	college-graduate, night extension, etc.

The youth market is a large one, containing nearly one half of the American population. The segment to be appraised here is the 19–25 year old age group and particularly the college market within this age group.

It is estimated that the U.S. college market consists of more than 8 million students enrolled in 2,374 institutions of higher learning. This market is a growing and relatively affluent segment of the general youth market. College students are estimated to purchase over $11 billion worth of goods and services each year. One way to appraise the college market in demographic and behavioral terms is to see if it can be further segmented—i.e., differentiated from other market targets so that appropriate variations may be made in product, promotion, or distribution policies.

However, understanding the demographics of the college market is not enough. For example, in approaching the college market marketers must consider such behavioral factors as:

1. College students are typically on an intellectual island, physically and behaviorally separated from other consumer groups.
2. Their world is dominated by emotional and intellectual pressures and ideas and ideals.
3. Their education and knowledge exceed those of any other generation at the same stage of development. This is not due to any innate intelligence differences but to the fact that today's young people are children of the "Technetronic era." Television has been a major influence in their lives; one estimate is that many young children watch over 8,000 hours of television prior to entering school.

Their social awareness and sophistication leads to identification and concern with social problems such as ecology, pollution, nutrition, minority group discrimination, and international relations. All of these characteristics foster an effort to establish identity within their peer group and to defend this group against "the Establishment." [26] Such insights can be useful in understanding the college market segment of the youth market. A similar type of demographic-behavioral analysis can be useful in serving other market segments and in assessing market opportunity.

Innovative marketers must continuously engage in the process of assessing marketing opportunity. They recognize that understanding the market and analyzing opportunities is most important and that the company that stops improving in opportunity assessment ceases being good at marketing.

[26] Much of the information on the college market in this chapter is from *The Youth Market: A Marketing Analysis* (New York: College Marketing Corporation, 1970).

4

MARKETING PLANNING FOR THE FIRM

Planning: The Basis of Marketing Management

Planning based on research and designed to achieve both customer satisfactions and corporate objectives is basic to the marketing concept. An integrated marketing strategy rests on a management philosophy that is based on planning. Because of its importance and complexity, planning, one of the enterprise functions of marketing management, is discussed in more detail in this section. Planning precedes market action and covers the business tasks that must be carried out before a program is made operational.

The need for financial and production planning has long been practiced in business; formal marketing planning, in the sense of giving systematic attention to careful calculation and coordination of corporate means and marketing ends is a relatively new development. Perhaps the key management concept here is the idea that concrete marketing objectives can be defined and a program of action designed to achieve them. Planning is not a luxury appendage of marketing, but a managerial element that is indispensable for the survival, growth, and profitable operation of the firm.

Any plan involving a change from existing patterns usually encounters substantial resistance. The task of the marketing executive managing change is to recognize the inevitable obstacles, provide ways of overcoming them in his planning, and see that the organization needed to implement the plan is structured to capitalize on the opportunities the plan is designed to meet. This requires drive and persistence from market planners comparable to the drive and persistence required of line executives.

Formal marketing planning is an integrative process which blends corporate goals and resources with information on opportunities external to the firm. The object of planning is to develop creative and innovative policies to guide corporate efforts in the marketplace. Successful planning involves combining information management and creative leadership to achieve marketing excellence and corporate goals.

PLANNING AS AN ENTERPRISE FUNCTION

Marketing planning includes the continuing managerial and technical activities and processes involved in assessing areas of marketing opportunity, determining the marketing mission and goals, developing and coordinating marketing action programs, and evaluating and adjusting all market-related programs. The first two elements of planning are essentially conceptual and analytical; the others are operational.

The enterprise functions of marketing planning are a natural extension and application to the current marketing situation of principles developed in the early history of the field. Henri Fayol, one of the earliest influential management thinkers, divided the field of administration into the elements of forecasting and planning, organization, commanding, coordinating, and controlling. He defined planning as both forecasting and providing a means of examining the future and drawing up a plan of action. A plan of action, according to Fayol, encompasses the goal, the line of action to be followed, the progressive stages, and the methods. He further said that the plan of action "is a kind of future picture wherein proximate events are outlined with some distinctness, whilst remote events appear progressively less distinct, and it entails the running of a business as foreseen, and provided over a definite period." [1]

LONG-RANGE PLANNING

The planning horizon in marketing is constantly being extended. Corporations in the United States are commonly and systematically planning five or more years into the future. In some of the major corporations, there is a trend to look ten and even twenty or twenty-five years ahead.

The long-range plan in a company operating under a planning philosophy can be very detailed. A two-inch-thick volume that attempts to forecast consumer buying patterns in 1980 serves as one map of the future for General Electric. In 1961 the United States Steel Corporation was estimating how much iron ore it will need in the year 2000. [2]

Effective long-range planning (LRP) requires coordinated planning in all functions and divisions of a firm. Prime consideration must be given to market and customer preference in the planning and decision-making of all departments that have a potential marketing impact. Because of the competitive necessity for LRP and improvement in the tools of LRP there is every reason to expect this trend to long-range planning to continue.

In most industries, rapid technological advances have been made in three areas of special interest to marketing planners—data processing

---

[1] Henri Fayol, *General and Industrial Management* (New York: Pitman Publishing Corp., 1949), p. 43. (Original published in French, 1909.)

[2] "More Companies Peer into Distant Future, Try to Prepare for It," *Wall Street Journal* (October 25, 1961), p. 1.

equipment, physical distribution concepts and facilities, and communications systems. Increasingly rigorous competition will force firms to make greater use of integrated automatic processes, combining manufacturing, physical distribution, and data processing. This integration may become a minimum basic requirement if a firm is to remain competitive. The magnitude of these changes and the investment required will vary with corporate objectives and skill in scientific long-range planning.

The trend is toward increased acceptance of marketing planning as a fundamental premise of business adjustment to present and future market patterns. As planning becomes a basic management technique and the cornerstone of management philosophy in designing marketing systems, practical methods of linking many market-related decisions and programs will be developed. The firm will be better able to capitalize on areas of market opportunity and profit, thereby achieving corporate goals in the market.

The planning concepts of mission, goals, objectives, and strategy are presented in this chapter. Also considered is the role of innovation in developing a dynamic, action-oriented, environmentally sensitive corporate entity.

Social System Orientation to Business Planning

During the 1960s many business executives used the marketing concept to help themselves become more responsive to consumers. The current thrust of corporate development is to move beyond the "marketing concept" to a social-system-oriented view of the firm as an integrated technological and marketing system.[3] In the spirit of this total systems approach to business, it is important to recognize business planning as a conscious decision-making network composed of complex and often uncertain information flows. Corporate mission, goals, objectives, and strategy are concepts implicit or explicit in all business decision-making.

These concepts can be differentiated by seeing them in the context of specific planning processes, a number of which have been developed in recent years.[4] Such an approach, however, is situation-specific and premature until a conceptual base applicable to most variations in business planning systems is developed.

Decisions generated from the assessment of marketing opportunities are blended to form a definition of the corporate mission and to determine current and projected goals of the business. Business objectives, the specific quantifiable ends toward which business activities are directed, are the foundations on which executives establish operational plans. Quantitatively stated objectives outlined in the plans guide specific business activities and programs within each functional business area. Figure 4-1

[3] Eugene J. Kelley, "Marketing Is a New Ball Game," *Sales/Marketing Today*, xvi, No. 4 (1970), 7–10.

[4] For example: Stanford Research Institute, "A Framework for Business Planning," *Business Week*, June 1, 1963, p. 54; Mark E. Stern, *Marketing Planning, A Systems Approach* (New York: McGraw-Hill, 1966), p. 13; David Luck and Arthur Preil, *Market Strategy* (New York: Appleton-Century-Crofts, 1968), pp. 4–5.

illustrates the broad planning framework. It indicates that the starting point of a discussion of the planning concept is the external environment in which the firm operates. The environment and changes in it provide the basis for defining and redefining the mission of the firm. Specific business goals are established and various functional objectives and strategies are designed to serve customers profitably.

MISSION OF THE FIRM

"Who is the company? What is the company?" [5] These questions must be answered not in terms of what the company is going to do, but in terms of what the company is going to be—to stockholders, to management, to customers, to distributors, to competitors, and to the rest of society? [6] These philosophical sounding questions are not nearly as esoteric as one might expect, for the answers to them provide the basis for business planning. They provide the firm with a "corporate mission and self-concept." Social psychologists have used the term "self-concept" to denote a "theory that attempts to explain the conception that the individual has of himself in terms of his interaction with those about him." [7] The basic propositions of the theory of self-concept, which can be adapted to the corporation by environmentally responsive business planners,[8] suggest:

1. The corporate "self-concept" is based on management perception of the way others (society) will respond to the corporation.
2. The corporate "self-concept" will function to direct the behavior of people employed by the company.
3. The actual response of others to the company will in part determine the corporate "self-concept." [9]
4. The "self-concept" is incorporated in statements of "corporate mission" in order for it to be explicitly communicated to individuals inside and outside the company—that is, for it to be actualized.

Historically, the firm has been viewed from an economic perspective. This orientation explains the debates in the 1950s and early 1960s regarding whether profit maximization, optimization, enterprise survival, or some other factor was the "goal/objective" of the company. Whether the term "goal" or "objective" was used proved of little importance at a time when economic guideposts, and profit consideration, were believed to be the

[5] Seymour Tilles, "The Manager's Job: A Systems Approach," *Harvard Business Review*, xli, No. 1 (January–February 1963), 75.

[6] H. Igor Ansoff, *Corporate Strategy* (New York: McGraw-Hill, 1965), p. 33.

[7] John W. Kinch, "A Formalized Theory of the Self-Concept," *The American Journal of Sociology*, lxviii (January 1963), 481–86.

[8] From Gilbert Harrell, "Company Mission, Goals, and Objectives" (unpublished manuscript, The Pennsylvania State University, March 1970).

[9] Kinch, *op. cit.*

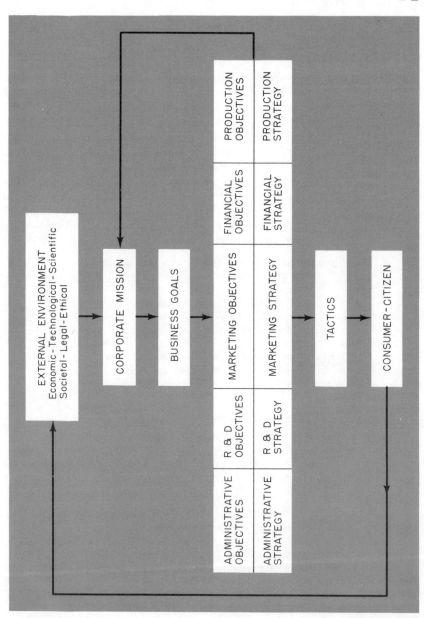

FIG. 4-1 Planning Framework

major basis of corporate policy. Today a social-environmental perspective is necessary to carry the company to a position of full contribution and growth. The term "corporate mission," with its broader connotations, is used to symbolize this highest level of company self-determination. For the firm, statements of "corporate mission" are essentially a qualitative, broad, basic, lasting, and innovative definition of the company.[10]

ORGANIZATIONAL GOALS

Corporate goals are broad, essentially qualitative, target components of planning. Many beginning business students believe that the basic goal of a business is profit making, and the marketing objective is to maximize sales volume. These are appealing but often dangerous notions; they lead to oversimplified and incorrect analyses of complex business problems. Profits are not so much a business goal as a condition necessary for survival and satisfactory economic performance. Profits reflect the social valuation of the firm's contributions to consumers. Profitability is the rationale of business enterprise, not its goal. Marketing effort is focused on customer service offered in the expectation of earning a profit. Goals, such as service, survival, and growth depend on profitable selling. If this is done effectively, the owners of the firm will receive profits, managers will receive salaries, and employees wages.

A challenging management task is that of obtaining a balance between short-term profits and long-term profitability. To do this managers must reconcile business goals, the present position and resources of the firm, profit requirements, and potential areas of long-run profit opportunity. Historically, corporate growth goals were achieved by introducing new models or new products to replace or supplement existing products. This has been a pattern of corporate growth throughout American business history. Today, however, the orderly introduction of new models of existing products is usually not enough to secure the growth goals of large firms. The current trend is toward a clear definition of corporate purposes, including plans for supplying a broader spectrum of customer wants and requiring strategies of diversification, acquisitions, and planned growth through serving new markets. The result is a corporate customer- rather than product-orientation.[11] Within this perspective goals are constrained by the corporate mission, but not the reverse.

Some general business goals that interact with corporate mission to form the basis of marketing strategy are:

> Survival of the firm or a subfirm organizational unit.
> Growth of the firm, division, product line, or product.

[10] Theodore Levitt explains "Marketing Myopia" as essentially a failure to properly identify and state "company mission." "Marketing Myopia," *Harvard Business Review*, xxxviii, No. 4 (August 1960), 45–56.

[11] "The Marketing Pattern: A Better Way for Business to Grow," *Business Week* (July 14, 1962), p. 60.

Short-term profit of the firm or product.
Long-run profit.
Enlargement of market size.
Maintenance or increase of market share.
Diversification of corporate activity.
Achievement of industry leadership.
Securing a balance between domestic and international business.
Maintaining employment at certain levels in particular plants.
Enhancement of image with various publics.

As this list suggests, the determination of profit and other goals is one of the most difficult conceptual tasks of management, and profit maximization is one of several, sometimes conflicting, business goals. This is particularly the case in the multidivisional, multiproduct, multinational business organization. Thus the modern corporation operates with a hierarchy of organizational and personal goals and objectives.

OBJECTIVES

Marketing objectives, and indeed any functional level objectives, relate to the firm's business goals, but are also designed to help fulfill its "corporate mission." [12] These objectives should be formulated in quantitative statements specifying what is to be accomplished. They should take into account the internal company situation through an interaction and evaluation of other functional objectives, a true systems perspective. Moreover, they should be analyzed and stated in terms of their relationship to the external environment.

Marketing objectives are statements of the corporate mission as operationalized for a specific time period. They are made specific with regard to market segments and customer needs. Marketing objectives focus corporate wide market related activities. Development of the marketing concept has moved business towards more in integrated functional areas. [13]

Determination of strategy and objectives is an important task for individuals as well as corporations. Robert Townsend states that, ". . . money, like prestige, if sought directly, is almost never gained. It must come as a by-product of some worthwhile objective . . . which is sought and achieved for its own sake." [14]

STRATEGY AND TACTICS

"Strategy," in the broadest sense, is a dynamic, action-oriented blueprint to accomplish "company mission," "business goals," and "functional objec-

[12] Norton Paley, "Corporate Objective and Marketing Aim: What is the Relationship?" *California Management Review*, xi, No. 2 (Winter 1968), 59–65.

[13] Robert Ferber, "Marketing Merging into a New Total Business Discipline," *American Marketing Association News* (May 1969), p. 1.

[14] Robert Townsend, *Up the Organization* (New York: Alfred A. Knopf, Inc., 1970), p. 62.

tives." Strategy "is the catalyst, the main thread and thrust of the business." [15] Most important, it is the bonding agent that provides the systematic directing force to actualize desired relationships between the firm and the environment. In the more specific contexts used throughout the business community, "strategy" has various shades of meaning, each of which leans toward the description given above but none of which touches it.

The different uses of the term "strategy" by prominent business authors center on how many of the policy-making and activity-directing processes are included in the definition. One common use of the term is in reference to corporate strategy, which has been defined as "the pattern of objectives, purposes, or goals and major policies and plans for achieving these goals, stated in such a way as to define what business the company is in or is to be in and the kind of company it is or is to be." [16] Such a broad definition could be considered the grand strategy of the business.

Confusion with the concept of strategy usually comes from two planes: (1) the failure to recognize it as a two-level function, and (2) the problem of differentiating it from "tactics." To complete the terminological profile, such a differentiation must be made explicit. "Strategy" is divided into concepts of "grand strategy" and "functional" (i.e., marketing) strategy. "Tactics" are an outcome of "functional strategy."

"Grand strategy" forms an interface with "company mission," "business goals," and "functional objectives." These elements form the result component of grand strategy, which is designed in response to them. Grand strategy is the integrating map that charts the development and use of resources to meet the challenges of fulfilling "corporate mission," "business goals," and "functional objectives."

Functional strategy, a middle management responsibility, grows out of grand strategy and is guided by the functional objectives. At the same time, alternative functional strategies and their probability of success are important inputs in deciding on "functional objectives." The two work as a bivariate subsystem within the larger system. Functional strategy (under the title of strategy) has been the topic of much research. Implicit in it are target components such as sales quotas by market segment and product line, quality control and so forth. [17]

The choice of mission, goals, objectives, and strategy is a simultaneous process involving patterns of information flows. The executive should focus his attention on the company's interaction with its environment, rather

[15] J. Thomas Cannon, *Business Strategy and Policy* (New York: Harcourt Brace Jovanovich, 1968), p. 3.

[16] Liddell Hart, a military strategy expert, provides a foundation for understanding the aberrations. "The role of 'grand strategy'—higher strategy—is to coordinate and direct all the resources of a nation, or band of nations towards the attainment of the political object of war. . . . Strategy (conventional) is the art of distributing and applying military means to fulfill the ends of policy. . . . Tactics lies in and fills the province of fighting. Strategy not only slaps on the frontier, but has for its purpose the reduction of fighting to the slenderest possible proportions." Liddell Hart, *Strategy* (New York: Frederick P. Praeger, 1954), pp. 336–47.

[17] Cannon, *Business Strategy and Policy*, p. 55.

than on factors primarily within the corporate framework. To achieve this end strategy designers should have considerable interaction with whatever management personnel set mission, goals, and objectives. In many instances both parties will be part of the same departmental team. Seymour Tilles commented on the difficulties of setting objectives when he wrote:

> The general state of the art of setting corporate objectives is an appalling one. By and large, the terms in which managers state their official aspirations are oversimplified deceptions: profit, market share, or return on investment. Each of these indicators still has great appeal to management, despite the extent to which scholars have rejected them as valid bases for performance evaluation. Their appeal lies primarily in the fact that each one sounds simple, since its inherent ambiguities are not obvious; each can be expressed in numbers, and thereby endowed with an aura of objectivity and utility; and each one can be a logical measure of past performance.
>
> The trouble with these criteria is that they entice the general manager to focus his attention where it does not belong: on the company itself, rather than on the relationship between the firm and the broader systems of which it is a part. This is vividly reflected in the design of the information systems. . . . Looking at these systems, one sees a great deal of money and effort devoted to analyzing what went on within the organization itself and very little, if anything, devoted to an analysis of environmental trends. Managers, too, frequently lose sight of the fact that corporate performance is the result of a company interacting with its environment, rather than the result of factors wholly within the company itself.[18]

"Tactics" are the day-to-day use of resources that have already been committed within a strategy. It is no longer a matter of deciding what or how much shall be committed; rather, it is a matter of assigning specific action to be taken, by whom, and when. Tactical planning in marketing directs the efforts of small groups or individuals and indicates the tactics and procedures to be used in a given marketing situation. A salesman may spend hours preparing his tactics for a half-hour sales interview. An advertising copywriter may spend several days on a particular piece of advertising copy. Anyone with management aspirations must first master the principles of tactical planning in his subfunction.

Having discussed corporate mission, goals, objectives, strategy, and tactics, we must ask: What differentiates the outstanding company from the also-rans? The answer is systematic corporate and marketing planning based on an innovative perspective geared to competitive action. The corporate strategic plan is the master plan that provides guidance to all managers about the direction in which the firm wants to go and the position it wants to achieve. This plan sets the boundaries for all other planning. Functional strategy is developed from grand strategy. Marketing strategy

---

[18] Tilles, *op. cit.*, p. 77.

is based on corporate marketing objectives (discussed above) and is implemented by a coordinated marketing action program. The ideal marketing strategy would achieve what military strategists refer to as a perfect economy of force. In economic terms, this would be the optimal strategy; that is, all resources of the firm, including personnel, would be utilized so that it would be impossible to improve the efficiency of one part of the operation without decreasing the effectiveness of others. With perfect economy of force the firm would correctly allocate resources, including money, to all marketing elements. But because of the nature of consumption and competition, particularly the uncertain human element, perfect economy of force represents an ideal rather than a practical planning goal.

A sharp division does not necessarily exist in practice between the levels and kinds of planning identified in the foregoing analysis. There is actually an interacting and reciprocal relationship between them, a hierarchy of plans in which corporate strategic planning influences tactical planning, and the results of planned tactical operations influence further corporate planning.

Innovation in Marketing Planning

A careful assessment of marketing opportunity will often result in some form of product or process innovation because in a competitive economic climate business growth and profit goals encourage innovation. As technology and life-style forces are related, businesses find that innovation is a function of growing importance and a basic measure of managerial competence. Innovation means the addition of something new and different to an existing situation. The new element can be a product, process, or intellectual contribution, such as a new concept. The managerial problem is one of planning and administering the injection of innovation on a systematic basis.

Figure 4–2 illustrates nine phases that are part of managing innovation in marketing.[19] In Phase 1 change is accelerating, normal, and constructive; this requires the discovery of unsatisfied market demands and the development of products and services to fill those demands. To cultivate opportunity and discover malfunctioning through research, technology, and comparison with existing products, services, and market wants and needs are the main function of Phase 2. Screening ideas to find the few that relate to the resources and mission of the company falls into Phase 3, while the identification of practical alternatives that might strengthen existing areas of weakness or lead to new areas of profitable opportunity is accomplished in Phase 4. Phase 5 identifies the courses of action to achieve the opportunities, and in Phase 6 the expected dollar value of each practical strategy is estimated. Phase 7, decision on innovation, is aided by previous

[19] See Eugene J. Kelley and William Lazer, "Managing Innovation in Marketing," *Advanced Management*, xxv (April 1960), 68–78, on which Fig. 4–2 and this section are based.

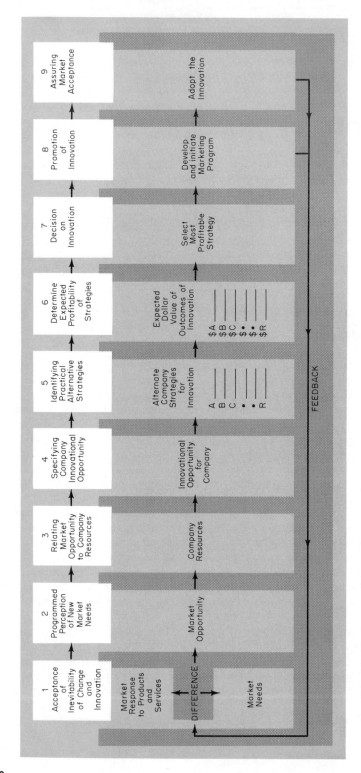

FIG. 4-2 The Process of Innovation

steps and other corporate considerations and objectives. Promotion of the innovation, Phase 8, occurs both inside and outside the firm. The last phase involves an improvement and refinement of the innovation from market information; it leads back to Phase 1 and recycling.

A major marketing challenge is stimulating the process of innovation and producing innovation in the amount required. This is largely a personnel-development and management problem. Segmenting our discussion of the innovation process permits ready identification of the contributions and talents of the many people required to produce and manage marketing innovation. The idea-generating aspects of innovation basically rest on the creative powers of a small group, although ideas by themselves are not necessarily valuable in business terms. The entrepreneur, the manager, the research technician, and the salesman are all parts of the total process of creating innovation and carrying it to an operational stage.

PRODUCT INNOVATION

The drug industry has long encouraged basic research. Drug research may be guided toward a firm's ideas of strength in order to relate new research knowledge to corporate resources and marketing opportunities. One drug company may have more successfully researched steroids than any competitor. Developing steroids will then present a special marketing opportunity for that company, and steroid drugs will be emphasized in its continuing research. If the company develops several products with a steroid compound, it must then determine, following the analysis suggested in Fig. 4–2, which steroid product presents the most profitable opportunity and is likely to deliver the greatest expected value. Drugs that are developed are then tested and marketed with a complete program. After promoting and distributing the product, the company may have to make adjustments in the product itself or in its form of presentation. These adjustments are based on information fed back from the market.

PROCESS INNOVATION

Innovation is also essential in the activities required to market goods and services efficiently. Recent process innovations include planned shopping centers, discount houses, physical distribution procedures, vending machines, and new organizational developments resulting from the marketing concept. The innovation process described in Fig. 4–2 operates in process as well as product situations.

The developers of shopping centers were among the first to recognize the marketing changes required to adapt to the evolving needs of Americans caught in the suburban population movement. These men recognized that changes in the population distribution and living style of suburban Americans meant that the existing retail structure located in the central business district of the metropolitan area could not serve consumers adequately. The area of marketing opportunity they visualized was further defined through various studies. When evidence supported the belief that existing concentrations of retail stores were not adequate to serve new market needs, these developers attempted to relate the unsatisfied needs to individual company or developer resources. In some cases, the developers were large department stores, such as J. L. Hudson in the Detroit metropolitan area. In other cases, real estate developers were the basic innovators.

Trends in Planning

The following trends summarize some of the developments described in this and preceding chapters. They represent planning trends currently under way which are expected to continue through the 1970s.

- Greater emphasis on marketing planning and sophisticated market research leading to the development of on-line marketing information systems to support an integrated, company-wide market-oriented effort.
- More environmental sensitivity in both domestic and international markets with more ability and communication channels to translate new customer needs into profitable action programs.
- More attention to market enlargement rather than market maintenance.
- An understanding of computer applications for market feedback and customer planning as structured marketing information systems develop.
- A demand for more precision, speed, and quality of analysis and decision-making forced by progress in management science and information technology.
- More concern with and research on the specific information needs of decision-makers.
- More attention to programmed innovation as a foundation for competitive advantage.

5

ORGANIZATION AND CONTROL
OF THE MARKETING EFFORT

Accurate assessments of marketing opportunity and careful planning are the bases for profitable business operation. Marketing plans cannot be fulfilled, however, until an organization has been assembled and personnel have been trained and motivated to implement the plans. It is not sufficient to think simply in organizational terms, for strong organizations have made poor plans work, and well-planned marketing programs have failed because of inadequate or improper controls. Effective marketing programs depend on the skill, technical competence, and vision of the planning group, the efficiency of organizational efforts, and on effective controls to achieve the established goals of the firm.

Kenneth Boulding stated the goals of organization and control as they relate to planning when he said, "What I think you can plan for is change itself. This is quite important. If you think in terms of an organization's flexibility in preparing for the unknown and of anticipating possible crises and systems changes, this really seems to me to be the essence of it." [1]

A market-oriented philosophy by top management is essential in preparing for the unknown future, for without it significant and competent programs at the operational level may be misdirected. The need to remain flexible in response to market forces provides the basis for planning the structure of the organization. Newer organizational approaches focus on business problems and human relationships, not on functions or departmental arrangements of business. Marketing managers are concerned with the use of resources to solve specific problems, such as optimizing profit, minimizing risk, developing customers, and increasing return on investment. Basically, a formal organization simply provides a structure in which people can efficiently perform tasks which will achieve corporate objectives.

Development of Marketing Organizations
in Manufacturing Firms

Historically, the development of marketing organizations can be seen as an adaptive process dealing with environmental change. During

---

[1] Kenneth E. Boulding, in a personal communication to the author.

the past century changes in the marketing organization have reflected the broader business moves from the industrial to the scientific revolution. Business orientation has changed from production, to sales, to consumers, and then to the centrality of marketing in an integrated business system. Each of these shifts has required different organizational forms, which are summarized in Table 5–1.

The study of organization is a complex matter. It is not possible to prescribe a perfect organization plan for all businesses—and perhaps not even for a single business at any point in time. Nevertheless, the organization chart can provide a convenient frame of reference for examining the evolution of organizational emphasis. Organization charts portray the formal structure of positions and working relationships in an organization; they do not illustrate the integration, coordination, and information flows existing among corporate personnel operating in a social system. Neither do they describe how decisions are actually made or the pattern of operation underlying given decisions.

The organization charts of two firms are rarely identical, for they reflect differences in factors relating to the mission of the firm, traditions, history, industry practices, and the character of each business. Organization charts do, however, illustrate standard practice at given points in the marketing development of industry. They provide a convenient device with which to relate major business developments to organization structures.

From a Production to a Marketing Orientation

Until about 1920, the essential marketing task in the United States was disposing of factory output, or selling. The organization was dominated by a production or financial orientation, with the sales department frequently placed under the manufacturing manager. Sales gradually gained in importance, and the typical organizational chart looked something like this:

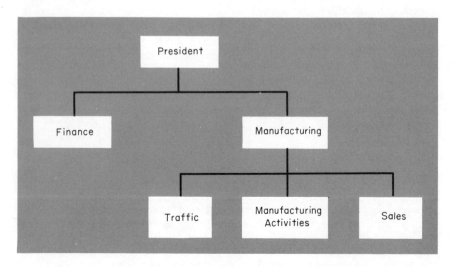

As competition intensified and selling was seen as more than soliciting orders, sales were removed from the production manager and given more management attention. The sales department came into existence, and supplementary selling functions developed which required more coordination. The company established a marketing research unit, which frequently reported to the sales manager. It also established an advertising department or strengthened an existing unit. Advertising was either under selling or, in some consumer-goods companies, a separate department. Merchandising or sales promotion was also established as a function. More aggressive promotion and selling characterized this period, and many efforts were made to make selling more "scientific." Sales selection and training techniques improved, but salesmen still operated with little or no staff support. The sales manager became more of a marketing executive but was rarely involved in corporate policy discussions. His primary concerns were still promotion and selling, with other functions viewed as supplemental. At this point, the organizational chart in many companies began to resemble the following:

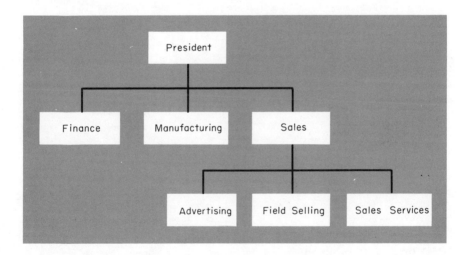

Faced with the changes identified in earlier chapters, firms reacted by broadening the definition of the firm's marketing mission. Sales departments broadened into marketing organizations, and new attention was given to product planning, pricing as a tool of competitive strategy, advertising, physical distribution, and marketing research. The functions of marketing planning were separated from operations, as indicated in the following organizational chart:

TABLE 5-1   Historical Development of Marketing Organizations

Approx. Period	Primary Problem	Orientation of Business Management	Management View of Marketing
1860–1919	Manufacturing and financial	Production and finance	Distribution
1920–1946	Manufacturing and distribution	Production and sales	Selling
1947–1959	Marketing	Customer	Prime business function
1960–1969	Systems integration	Technology and marketing	Control function in an integrated business system
1970s	Societal relationships	Systems— Metamarketing	Social-Managerial Process

TABLE 5-1 *(cont.)*

Major Business Developments	Organizational Responses in Marketing

Continuation of Industrial Revolution
Closing of the Frontier in 1890
Growth of large-scale firms
Scientific management movement
Rise of mass production, scientific agriculture
Increasing government regulation
Dominance of the large city over retailing
Distribution and selling subordinate to
    manufacturing but growing in importance
	Field selling emphasis
	Advertising sections established
	Beginning of formal marketing
	    research

Mass markets and national companies
Transportation-communications technology
    improvement
Great Depression, problems of scarcity and
    surplus production
Supermarkets, self-service
Excess production capacity becomes char-
    acteristic
Government regulation of markets and
    marketing
	Growth of sales management
	Increased nonpersonal promotion
	Advertising, sales promotion, and
	    public relations
	Growth of staff functions
	Marketing research depts. increase
	Shift from sales managers to general
	    sales executives

Knowledge explosion in technology
Acceleration of life-style changes by
    consumers
Shopping centers, discount selling
Affluent society and substitute product
    competition
Increased importance of international
    business
Concept of marketing as a system
	Product managers
	Vice-presidents of marketing
	International Divisions
	Physical distribution managed as
	    marketing function
	Increased marketing planning

More scientific decision making in business
Growing sense of social responsibility
Integration of marketing functions and
    business policy
Rising expectations of consumers
	Marketing voice in basic questions of
	    corporate policy
	More presidents with view of business
	    as a consumer-satisfying organiza-
	    tion
	Emergence of multinational enterprises

Increased computer usage
New decision processes
Integration of all business functions
A new conceptual framework for business
A social systems orientation
	A systems emphasis beyond a mar-
	    keting orientation
	Emergence of better control through
	    computers and quantitative tech-
	    niques

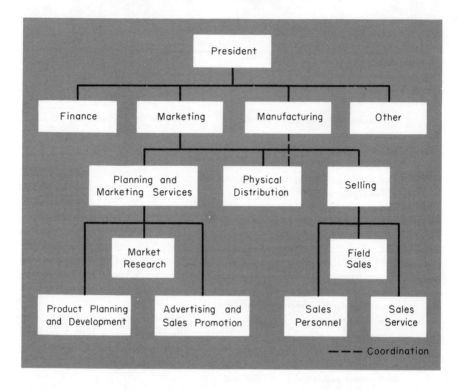

Few companies have followed these exact patterns of departmental organization, although the trends are correctly indicated. For instance, in corporate policy-making the marketing viewpoint is increasingly represented by a major marketing executive, frequently a vice president. In the earlier stages of business development, the executive committee of most companies consisted of the president, the production manager, and the controller. The sales manager was a middle-management officer, and was rarely expected to contribute to basic corporate policy.

A marketing-minded company not only views selling as a key marketing activity, but also emphasizes the research and planning activities that form the basis of effective selling. This point of view stresses profit, not necessarily volume. The next stage of development is to recognize the veto power of the market over a wide variety of corporate policy decisions.

By the 1960s an understanding of the marketing concept had been reached which encouraged management to view the total enterprise and its objectives, functions, and organization. Broadly stated, the systems approach views the firm as an integrated whole. Problem-solving and planning focus upon the entire organization and its goals rather than on functional areas, such as sales or distribution.

The achievement of business goals is determined in large measure by the ability of marketing executives to understand and meet change in people, markets, and the environment in which the firm operates. Information technology and other scientific processes have catalyzed change in almost every element of modern life. It is through managing change, congruent with customer values, that marketers are able to contribute to company goals. Management ideas and practices in all business functions will continue to change as technology and society change. Therefore marketing, as the business function most concerned with the generation and completion of economic transactions and with the management of change, is itself characterized by continuous change.

PILLSBURY COMPANY

The effect of environmental change upon the objectives and operation of a company can be illustrated by a close examination of one particular company. Four distinct phases in business organizations are evident in the development of marketing in the Pillsbury Company.[2]

Production Orientation—The Pioneering Era. The Pillsbury Company was formed in 1869. In its early years, the primary concern of Mr. Charles A. Pillsbury, founder, was with production and manufacturing. The main problem of most businesses was to produce products to fill the needs of the westward-expanding country. The company philosophy in this era might have been stated thus: "We are professional flour millers. Blessed with a supply of the finest North American wheat, plenty of water power, and excellent milling machinery, we produce flour of the highest quality. Our basic function is to mill high-quality flour, and, of course (and almost incidentally), we must hire salesmen to sell it, just as we hire accountants to keep our books."

Sales Orientation—The Second Era. The next stage of development was the sales era, which Pillsbury entered in the 1930s. At this time, Pillsbury, like other consumer-goods companies, began to become conscious of consumer wants, preferences, and habits as being the key factors in business planning. Thus the company established a commercial research department with the goal of obtaining relevant facts about the market. It formally recognized the role and importance of wholesale and retail food merchants as key links in the distribution of its products from the mill to homes. With these two developments the company took a major step along the road to becoming marketing-oriented. Pillsbury's thinking in this second era could be stated as follows: "We are a flour-milling company, manufacturing a number of products for the consumer market. We must have a first-rate sales organization that can dispose of all the products we can make at a favorable price. We must back up this sales force with consumer advertising and market intelligence. We want our salesmen and our dealers to have all the tools they need for moving the output of our plants to the consumer."

---

[2] The Pillsbury material is adapted from the *Journal of Marketing*, in an article by Robert J. Keith, "The Marketing Revolution," xxiv, No. 1 (January 1960), 35–38.

Marketing Orientation—The Third Era. Pillsbury executives feel the company did not enter the marketing era until 1960. The stimulus was the spectacular growth of Pillsbury's baking mixes, and the growing realization that technical research and production facilities were capable of producing literally hundreds of new and different food products. The company faced the need to determine specific new products and required criteria for selecting the kinds of new products to develop and manufacture. This required an organization to plan and sell the products selected.

With these needs in mind, Pillsbury decided to build into the company a new management function that would plan, direct, and control the work of other corporate departments with market needs. This meant integrating activities from purchasing and production through advertising and sales. The Marketing Department was established to perform these functions. The new department developed criteria from consumers' needs, which could be used in determining which products to make and market. The company's philosophy in the period of marketing orientation could be stated: "We make and sell products for consumers."

Marketing Control—The Fourth Era. This stage can be summarized in company terms as: "We are moving from a company that has the marketing concept to a marketing company." Marketing is now recognized as basic to the development of long-range company policy. The significant organizational change is the integration of marketing with top-management decision-making. In the third stage marketing set short-term operating policies, but as the fourth era of marketing control progresses, marketing will become the basic motivating force for the entire corporation. This means that every activity of the corporation will be aimed at satisfying consumer needs and desires.

After reviewing Pillsbury's marketing evolution, the question can be asked, "What comes next?" Is marketing control the ultimate stage? History suggests otherwise. It is possible to speculate that the next stage might involve viewing an organization as an integrated business and technological system aimed at satisfying consumption needs. This view requires blending marketing and technological capacity and is a natural extension of the marketing concept. A clue to Pillsbury's thinking in this area is the appointment of a Vice President of Growth and Technology to integrate the technical development of new products with the marketing aspects of product planning. In the years ahead, more companies will move in this direction, developing an organization that focuses all resources of the firm on market needs and opportunities.[3]

---

[3] Students of dynamic disciplines tend to become immersed in contemporary problems and neglect the study of the roots and history of a field. Each generation must, to some extent, define marketing according to its needs. The study of the past, however, can provide a perspective and understanding of contemporary problems. Marketing scholars are now remedying the neglect of the historical approach: One of the fields of growth in marketing is in the area of marketing history and thought. The sources and development of marketing thought, with emphasis on the period 1900–1960, are discussed in Robert Bartels, *The Development of Marketing Thought* (Homewood, Ill.: Richard D. Irwin, Inc., 1962).

A Systems View of Organization

Three systems notions useful in studying marketing organization are those of *input, output,* and *communications feedback.* The manager of a marketing system must identify and collect the various resources, or inputs, required to accomplish the specific goals, or systems output, desired. Inputs and outputs are linked through the flow of information moving through and around a marketing organization. The interdependence of the inputs and the information that flows between the complex, interacting, but separately organized, functions of marketing, research and development, production, and finance is growing, as is the interdependence of the subfunctions of marketing.

In addition to systems analysis, the student of marketing organization must become familiar with the concepts of authority, responsibility, delegation, accountability, and line and staff. Familiarity with these concepts is a prerequisite to understanding the organizational structures and procedures summarized below: [4]

1. *Determine the objectives of the organization.* This involves company-wide objectives. At the departmental level, specific departmental objectives must be determined within the overall company objective and policy.
2. *Determine the action needed to accomplish these objectives.* This involves determining the work involved, describing each specific job that is to be performed, and developing a job analysis and job specifications for each job.
3. *Determine how the objectives can be accomplished.* This involves establishing basic policies as guides to action, isolating the primary policy responsibilities for marketing, and formulating policies for each area as a guide to those who will actually do the job.
4. *Determine the kind of organization needed for the job.* This means determining the kinds of job groupings that should be developed to do the best possible job. Here, organizational charts are useful to indicate the flow of authority and to establish relationships as they exist in the organization both vertically and horizontally.
5. *Determine the number and kind of people needed to do the necessary jobs.* It is at this point that managers are concerned with problems of recruiting, selection, training, compensation, supervision, and evaluation of workers.

Acceptance of the systems approach requires shifts in organizational forms and in the assignment of responsibility. The systems view of organization, which is currently more an ideal than an applied activity, is being utilized by firms to design and organize marketing activities. These designs generally include three kinds of organizational mechanisms that are

[4] Adapted from Hector Lazo and Arnold Corbin, *Management in Marketing* (New York: McGraw-Hill Book Company, 1961), p. 76.

basic to the systems view of marketing—the customer or market direction in non-marketing decision areas must be introduced; the shift to general marketing management must be made; and marketing must be coordinated with the other functions of the company.[5]

The current trends in marketing organization reflect two main elements. First, business functions formerly considered to be non-marketing are being assigned to marketing, or at least are being coordinated with marketing; product development and physical distribution are two examples. Second, other functions, such as marketing research, have been upgraded in importance. An organizational trend that is expected to continue is the involvement of non-marketing executives in decision-making that has consumer implications and the inclusion of marketing executives in planning for areas traditionally considered non-marketing.

The broader organizational consequences of the marketing concept may lead to the development of the "marketing company," a term used to describe a basic way of business thinking. The responsibilities of marketing executives, including salesmen, are different under the marketing concept from what they once were. The marketing philosophy of business is influencing the way non-marketing executives view and perform their tasks, as evidenced by the integration of the reciprocal relations between technological research and marketing.

For peak efficiency, a balance must be maintained between the strengths and capabilities of the functional groups of the organization. Yet many firms have not achieved this balance. David Moore points out that the social anthropologist tends to concentrate on functional interdependency and views society as a kind of living system that maintains a certain equilibrium or balance among its diverse segments.[6] Like the anthropologist, the manager must also view his organization as an evolving social and technological system.

Control: A Systems View

Achievement of equilibrium in a sociotechnical system is provided by various control mechanisms. Effective control, however, demands adaptation to environmental changes so that external, as well as internal, balances are maintained. The organization is constantly subjected to competing demands from internal sources—i.e., functional areas—and external sources—i.e., competitors and consumers—which must be integrated and balanced. Thus the marketing organization should be viewed as an open system in which resources or inputs are assembled from the environment, and outputs in the form of information, products, and services are returned to the environment.

[5] Edward C. Bursk, *Text and Cases in Marketing: A Scientific Approach* (Englewood Cliffs, N.J.: Prentice-Hall, Inc., 1962), p. 498.

[6] David G. Moore, "Marketing Orientation and Emerging Patterns of Management and Organization," in *Managerial Marketing: Perspectives and Viewpoints,* Eugene J. Kelley and William Lazar, eds., 3rd ed. (Homewood, Ill.: Richard D. Irwin, Inc., 1967), p. 352.

Control of the marketing effort requires planning for the correct information and material inputs needed to obtain the output required to satisfy the needs of consumers. The policies associated with product promotion, and distribution will be introduced here, with detailed discussion to follow in Chapter 6.

EXTERNAL CONTROL

To maintain equilibrium with respect to environmental forces, the firm must be able to quickly adapt to disturbances and changes in the environment. Modifications of the firm's output lead to further environmental changes, which in turn may influence further change in the market forces in a perpetuating cycle. Effective adaptation to change can only be accomplished through the utilization of feedback to evaluate strategies. Thus, an intelligence network must be maintained which will enable the firm to detect and analyze both change in the environment and the forces at work which promote such change. The design of such intelligence systems is an integral part of the planning process and holds implications for the organization structure and control mechanisms.

INTERNAL CONTROL

The effectiveness of marketing programs hinges on leadership, which should begin at the top and flow throughout the entire company. The chief executives of the company, including the chairman of the board and the president, should be considered leaders of the marketing team. Only then can the systems approach be fully functioning and the spirit of meta-marketing be felt by all members of the organization.

The marketing function places a premium on those individuals who are capable of motivating and directing people to enthusiastic action. The emotional and human relations aspects of marketing cannot be neglected by marketing managers. An understanding of human relations is important when dealing with customers and salesmen, and in designing promotional campaigns for both consumer and industrial markets.

A logical, balanced, fact-founded plan is likely to be executed more effectively if it recognizes the human intangibles in a marketing organization, particularly the key role of leadership. The complexities of marketing management are increasing, and the competitive and personal pressures of executive leadership are growing more intense. For example, the use of computers is beginning to change the whole approach to information management in marketing. Just as marketing executives will learn to appreciate and utilize computers and computer specialists as the problems of information management increase, they will probably also have to develop their knowledge and skills in the behavioral area, including skills in personal leadership and human relations. Other intellectual demands that did not exist a few years ago are also being made on leadership. For example, problems of international marketing and the need for integrating marketing with technology, business policy, and changing marketing patterns offer complexities that were not faced by executives in the past and that place new demands on marketing leadership.

The increasing complexity of marketing organizations is fostering a new interest in the human relations aspects of the marketing system. At times, human relations skill seems at least as important as technical proficiency. Marketing poses special human relations problems because of the nature of its tasks. The penalties or rewards in human relations appear greater and more immediate in the marketing field than in business activities not so directly concerned with the public. In marketing, the costs of poor human relations policies are usually translated quickly into lost business; in production, they are not so immediately apparent, although it is possible to detect them. Poor labor relations, as measured by strikes and slowdowns, may be as costly to the company as poor human relations in marketing.

The special responsibility for maintaining and improving external relations, particularly with customers, explains the particular importance and complexity of human relations in marketing.

All managers have the task of working through people; all effective managers recognize individual differences in people, both employees and customers, for the same appeals are not equally effective with all. A successful marketing manager perceives much of his job in human relations terms and is concerned with maximizing the productivity of individuals and groups under his jurisdiction and influence through effective human relations. He recognizes the corporate investment in a marketing organization and the competitive necessity of securing a high return on the manpower investment.

Managing any group of people poses many common problems, regardless of each group's specific objectives. Responsibility and authority relationships must be defined, policies established, communications made effective, coordination secured, people motivated, conflicts reconciled, and people appraised, rewarded, or sanctioned. In all departments of a firm the manager has the task of encouraging a creative and imaginative approach and supplanting conflict with cooperation.

The dimensions of the marketing task and the perspectives of individuals of many backgrounds in the marketing system account for many of the problems. Differences between groups may emerge from the differences in the missions and functions of the groups in which people work; the similarities may stem from the basic biogenic and psychogenic characteristics of people in any organization. The task of balancing these complex conflicting needs and drives in an organization comes close to being the heart of management in marketing or any other field.

Organization and Control: Planning Perspectives

Mechanisms of organization and control must be planned to adapt to change, as is seen in the following comment:

The economies of the United States, Canada, and Western Europe will increasingly be dominated by large, highly diversified, multinational corporations at all levels of manufacturing and distribution. The marketing problems of these corporations will differ from those of traditional companies that operate on a more limited scale within a narrower range of products, markets, and production stages.[7]

In both organization and control the difficult managerial task is balancing the procedural and mechanical expertise with factors of human motivation and performance.

MANAGERIAL CONTROL

Marketing control is both a process and a concept. It is part of the process of management, and, in systems terms, it is indivisible from planning and organization. Control is a continuous and pervasive process of establishing standards, measurement of performance, comparison, evaluation, and adjustment of marketing policies, programs, and procedures. The modern concept of marketing control is that it consists of more than the measurement and audit function; it is both diagnostic and prognostic. In part, control is utilized to secure the most efficient use of financial, human, and physical resources consistent with the firm's objectives. The results of marketing effort are compared to programmed objectives and to changed conditions in order to measure and secure progress toward planned results. Profit goals are critical control centers under the marketing concept.

In addition to indicating whether operating results conform to the plans made, control is fully utilized when it can be used to provide the basis for modifying plans and predicting optimal future courses of action. Control is, therefore, a recycling of the planning process to provide the adaptive response needed.

Controls should also be used in both goal setting and goal seeking to achieve the ultimate control objective of appropriately responding to change. The ultimate objective of control in marketing is not to measure results, but to motivate and direct an organization and individuals toward optimal efficiency.

Effective control requires integrated management skills in planning the goal setting, establishing performance standards, comparing results against standards, utilizing motivational and measurement devices and procedures, and adjusting programs on a results basis. When results differ from standards, programs must be realigned and resources reallocated to bring performance to the parameters desired.

The customer is the ultimate controller of marketing and firm operations; he controls many corporate programs and holds veto power over all marketing programs described in the following chapters.

[7] Robert D. Buzzell, "What's Ahead for Marketing Managers?" *Journal of Marketing*, xxxiv, No. 1 (January 1970), 3.

ORGANIZATION FOR MARKETING INFORMATION SYSTEMS

Marketing information systems have evolved in response to the organizational need for information flows and in response to the increased complexity of collecting, synthesizing, and routing proper information to marketing decision-makers. Information systems combine both technological and organizational skills to yield an integrated medium for the communication of knowledge throughout the organization. In most companies failure to develop a good system is more the result of organizational constraints than of inadequate technological capabilities.

Conrad Berensen has defined a marketing information system as "an interacting structure of people, equipment, methods and controls which is designed to create an information flow that is capable of providing an acceptable base for management decisions in marketing." [8] As such, the operation of a marketing information system involves the efforts of the following individuals and departments: [9]

- Top Management
- Marketing Management and Branch Management
- Sales Management
- New Product Groups
- Market Research Personnel
- Control and Finance Departments
- Systems Analysts and Designers
- Operations Researchers, Statisticians, and Model Builders
- Programmers
- Computer Equipment Experts and Suppliers

Conceptually, the information system is composed of four major internal components requiring a coordinated staff: [10] (1) A data bank, (2) a measurement-statistics bank, (3) a model bank, and (4) a communications capability. The four internal components interact with (1) the decision-making network and (2) the environment, as is shown in Fig. 5–1.

The design and implementation of a marketing information system are a long-term and often costly undertaking.[11] However, a company fully organized to satisfy customer wants will find it is in a good position to develop a functioning information system. The importance of information

[8] Conrad Berensen, "Marketing Information Systems," *Journal of Marketing,* xxxiii, No. 4 (October 1969), 16.

[9] Richard H. Brien and James E. Stafford, "Marketing Information Systems: A New Dimension for Marketing Research," *Journal of Marketing,* xxxii, No. 3 (July 1968), 22.

[10] From David B. Montgomery and Glen L. Urban, "Marketing Decision-Information Systems: An Emerging View," *Journal of Marketing Research,* vii (May 1970), 226–34.

[11] David B. Montgomery, "Developing a Balanced Marketing Information System," working paper, Marketing Science Institute, July 1970.

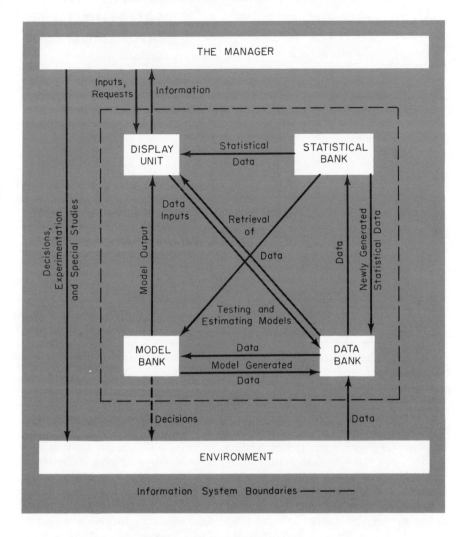

FIG. 5-1   Decision-Information System Structure

Source: Montgomery and Urban, "Marketing Decision-Making Information Systems: An Emerging View," *Journal of Marketing Research,* vii (May 1970), 227.

flows and experience in handling them will have already evolved out of efforts to satisfy customers profitably. Alternatively, the company that has failed to recognize the importance of customer satisfaction and innovation will find the information system concept relatively difficult to implement. Such a firm will find it necessary to bolster the organization with more enlightened personnel before it can begin such an undertaking. At the same time, the introduction of such a system should, if properly designed, foster more effective marketing.

6

PRODUCT POLICY AND
THE MARKET OFFER

Two important components of marketing strategy are (1) a definition of market targets, including the types of customers the firm wishes to reach; and (2) "composition of a marketing mix."[1] Market targets delineate the specific objectives established after the assessment of marketing opportunity and the determination of the corporate mission and marketing objectives. The marketing mix is the combination of manpower and other resources and inputs needed in marketing programs to fulfill objectives and plans in the marketplace.

The marketing mix can be viewed as the firm's total market offering, consisting of the product, including physical characteristics and price, the logistical support, packaging, company image, advertising, and promotion. Since consumers perceive the output of the firm in the form of the product or service, the marketing strategist must integrate all the elements when determining strategy.

However, the marketing mix is even more than the sum of product characteristics, price, promotion, and distribution. As is illustrated in Fig. 6–1, a synergistic quality evolves from these elements to give a product or product line an image. This image is the perception customers and potential customers have of the firm's offerings in terms of their unique needs. Using this perspective, the marketer realizes that altering one element of the marketing mix necessarily affects the impact of the other variables. For example, magazine advertising may be worthless for promoting personally tailored products or services, such as insurance, unless it is accompanied by adequate personal selling. At the same time, highly standardized consumer goods, such as detergents or stockings, may respond well to magazine advertising or direct mail, but may represent too low a volume per item for personal selling.

---

[1] See Alfred R. Oxenfeldt, "The Formulation of a Market Strategy," in *Managerial Marketing: Perspectives and Viewpoints*, Eugene J. Kelley and William Lazer, eds. 3rd ed. (Homewood, Ill.: Richard D. Irwin, Inc., 1967), pp. 98–108.

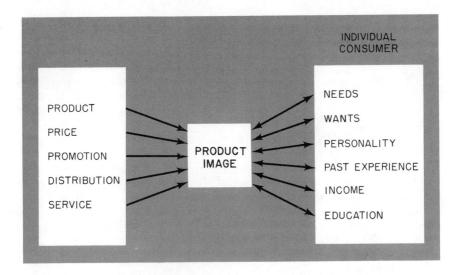

FIG. 6-1   Product Image Formation

Each of the marketing-mix elements is discussed separately in the following analysis. While this approach is conceptually convenient, the reader should remember that it is the creative combination of these elements that yields the proper integrated strategy.

Product Policy

Product policy decisions form an important basis for the firm's competitive advantage and are, therefore, central to all marketing. An integrated product policy and planning effort draws on the resources and talents of all functional areas of the company. Therefore, non-marketing executives are involved in product decisions along with marketing executives. The common purpose is the development of a process of conscious effort toward matching products, within the firm's resource capabilities, to the needs, wants, and environments of the marketplace in order to attain the goals of the firm. For example. Volkswagen's successful penetration of the U.S. auto market can be linked to its serving the consumer's need for a sub-compact car, which was not being met by American auto makers. Thus, product policy decisions become the focal point of a firm's marketing program because product characteristics and decisions shape marketing decisions in pricing, promotion, distribution, and, to a great extent, establish the company posture as seen by consumers.

In successful enterprises such as Ford Motor Company, General Foods, and IBM, marketing and product research go hand in hand. Companies that understand fully the concepts of good marketing have marketing-oriented personnel and executives making product development decisions in the earliest phases of product research. Marketing decisions determine the avenues of new product searches as well as the extent to which product ideas, once born, will be further developed. The extent to which the marketing orientation is accepted by a company is indicated by the level at which marketing analysis enters product development decisions. The involvement of marketing people in the setting of broad research directions is one indication of a corporate marketing philosophy. If marketing people do not become involved until after a product or product idea has been developed, it is quite possible the company lacks market-oriented management.

The impact of product decisions reaches far beyond marketing into many other major corporate levels and functions, including direction of the firm's technological research programs, resource development programs, and long-range growth plans. From a marketing viewpoint, the firm's competitive advantage in the marketplace rests fundamentally on product policy decisions properly integrated with other elements of marketing and over-all corporate strategy.

History is replete with examples of product failures resulting from developments which lacked marketing insight. One example from the drug industry was a chewable, cherry-flavored cold tablet which tasted so good that consumers did not believe it to be effective. A second example of product failure was a cold capsule, that, while excellent in preventing colds from spreading to many parts of the respiratory system, failed to relieve a major and distressing symptom of the cold syndrome.

The addition of new products, the modifications or abandonment of existing products, and the entry into new markets with new or established products are business problems that require a great deal of knowledge to resolve effectively. The manager concerned with these decisions has four resource areas to consider when formulating product policy. These can be broadly classified as physical, human, financial, and market. (See Table 6–1.) All factors must be carefully considered and developed to achieve an innovative product policy.

PRODUCT MANAGER

The complexities of product management have led to the appearance of a new marketing executive, the product manager, who coordinates company marketing and sales efforts for a particular product or product line. The product manager typically reports to a vice president of marketing.

The product manager's job involves both marketing research and planning, and requires a good grasp of marketing management theory. In addition, he must work with sales and advertising managers to see that his product gets its full share of the coordinated corporate effort.

David Luck has termed product managers the "vital organizational loci for the focus of marketing interfaces." [2] According to studies involving

[2] David J. Luck, "Interfaces of a Product Manager," *Journal of Marketing*, xxxiii, No. 4 (October 1969), 33.

TABLE 6-1   Selected Resource Areas in Product Policy

Physical Resources	Human Resources	Financial Resources	Market Resources
Manufacturing facilities	Salesmen, engineers, skilled labor	Money available for financial research and development, construction inventory, etc.	Brand preferences or loyalty
Raw material reserves, ownership, or preferential access	Professional leaders with skill, experience, ambition, and managerial talents	Working capital	Existence of actual or potential customers
			Market contracts
Warehouses, ships, trucks, etc.			Market goodwill or confidence
			Acceptability

twenty-six product managers, the important interfaces with which the product manager interacts are: the buying public, distributors, sales force, advertising agencies, product development teams, and marketing research teams.[3] In effect, the product manager first develops a strategic marketing plan for the product and then coordinates and motivates sales managers, salesmen, advertising people, distribution management, and product researchers to carry out appropriate implementing tactics. This requires exceptional skills in interpersonal relations because the product manager usually has only informal control over these individuals or departments in the organization.

PRODUCT LIFE CYCLE

Traditionally, dynamic growth industries are built upon and sustained by an orderly and consistent flow of new products. Such product innovation will become more critical in the future as scientific advances are made at greatly increased rates. For example, IBM has regularly updated and advanced its computers and support systems to keep pace with expanded knowledge in the information processing field.

A product, once introduced, passes through five stages of what is called its product life cycle before its eventual abandonment. These phases can be illustrated by the following sales curve, Fig. 6–2.

[3] Ibid.

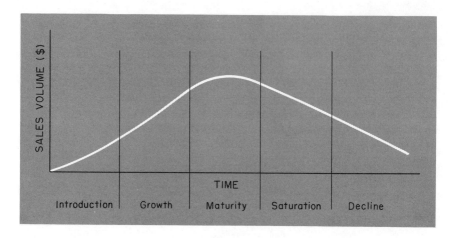

FIG. 6-2 Sales Curve

Introduction occurs when the product enters the market for the first time. This is usually accompanied by high promotion investments, elaborate feedback programs, and adjustments in the marketing strategy.

Growth is the phase characterized by rapid consumer acceptance for products which survive the introductory phase. It is at this stage that the firm should begin thinking about new uses and new markets for the product.

Maturity follows the rapid sales growth of the second phase. At the end of this stage the market has reached a peak of acceptance; sales and usefulness have begun to approach peak profitability.

Saturation occurs when competitors copy, improve, or otherwise undermine a product's popularity.

Decline is typified by decreasing sales. The product will probably have to be replaced with new products because the product is losing its market position. Concern with customers may center on service.

Although product life cycle is a normal and important business phenomenon, it may be more practical to study the profit curve in Fig. 6–3, because high sales volume does not automatically imply high profits.

In today's rapidly changing environment profit usually peaks at the end of the growth stage and begins to decline during maturity. New product introductions at regular and frequent intervals are often the only means to continue profitability.

EXTENDING THE PRODUCT LIFE CYCLE

Figure 6–3 reinforces an earlier statement that the corporation should begin investigating new markets, products, or uses in the growth phase of rapid consumer acceptance. It can be anticipated that shortly after this

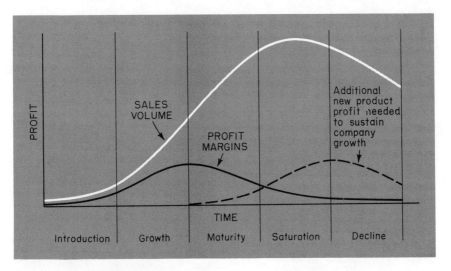

FIG. 6-3   Basic Life Cycle of Products

Source: Management Research Department, Booz-Allen & Hamilton Inc.

rapid growth the profit curve normally will begin to decay despite the shape of the sales curve.

The life of American Motors' Rambler is a good example of a product which reached the saturation point when the company was not ready to capture new markets or withstand competition from the big three auto makers. Without new models and new campaigns, the company found it could not maintain a market position; and only through an extremely trying period of liquidations and cutbacks was American Motors able to stay in business.

Management can, in some cases, find methods of countering the obsolescence trend short of new product development. Corporate mergers are one possible alternative for firms losing their market positions and, barring government intervention, the 1970s should see much of this.

Another possibility is the development of new uses for existing products. For example, one now finds nylon and fiberglass in practically any form. Another good example is the expansion of the greeting card business. Both traditional and contemporary cards are available for most occasions and many for no occasion at all. Kerosene, which might have become obsolete with the harnessing of electrical power, is popular now as a source of heat and light for summer cottages and tents, as a fuel for portable cook-stoves and racing boats.

Probably the largest, yet least tapped, of these alternatives is the international marketplace. The world's current population is roughly 3 billion and increasing. This represents a huge potential market for the far-sighted and enterprising manager. Rising world affluence and the increasing number of emerging nations create an international purchasing power of staggering proportions. In many nations the average citizen has the means to consume more than he does, for his country's economy is still geared to the production of capital rather than consumer goods. People in these emerging nations readily purchase products which are passively accepted in the United States.

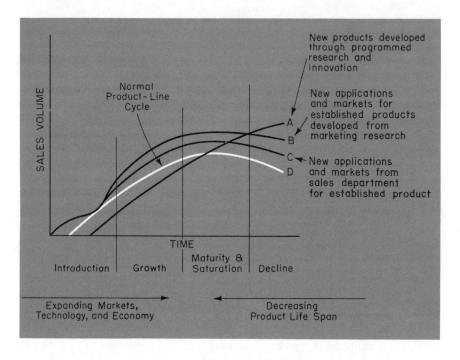

FIG. 6-4 The Life Cycle of Successful New Products

Figure 6–4 illustrates the ways to extend the basic product life cycle. This is shown by the upward movement of the curve represented by A, B and C in Fig. 6–4 as superimposed over D—the normal product line life cycle. Such applications can only extend the normal line up to a point. Ultimately, new products must be introduced. These can take the form of model changes or an entirely new product line. Assessment of the product's position in the product line life cycle is essential, because market plans and strategies vary with this position. Product, pricing, promotion, and distribution strategies appropriate for the introductory stages of a product normally will not be optimal for other stages.

Life cycle analysis helps identify the stages of development for different products in a firm's product and communications mix and may then indicate the need for reallocation of resources. A product in the later stages may require substantial modification through product redesign, or it may have to be eliminated from the line.

NEW PRODUCT DEVELOPMENT

Years of study and consulting experience have led the management consulting firm of Booz-Allen & Hamilton to the following convictions regarding new products:

1. New products are basic to company growth and survival—more so now than ever before.
2. The evolution of new products is not an abstract mystery. It is a practical business function that can best be described as a management process.
3. The new product program of a company must be organized and controlled if it is to be managed effectively.[4]

Developing ideas for new products is not easy. The approach to innovation management presented in Chapter 4 suggests the general ways in which product ideas may be developed from multiple sources. Committees use various methods in attempting to answer questions on the suitability of new products. Efforts are made to quantify the information in the form of mathematical models and to arrive at a numerical evaluation of the best product choice. Other methods are essentially subjective and seem to be a matter of business judgment, relating product opportunities to corporate goals after considering questions such as these: [5]

What is the profit contribution picture?
Will the present channels of distribution be compatible?
Will the present product line be complemented by the addition of this product?
Will it stimulate or adversely affect sales of current products?
Does the product possess distinctive characteristics which will allow ease of promotion?
What is the expected life cycle of the product?
What is the size of the potential market for this product?
Will it be affected by cyclical or seasonal variations?
Can it be produced using existing plant facilities?

Effective product strategy usually requires the integration of new products with existing products and with the marketing and manufacturing capabilities of the firm. Successful product campaigns have resulted from deliberate attempts to develop products that use the company's special resources and management skills, including existing facilities and established distribution channels.

The Whirlpool Corporation is an example of a company that has broadened its product mission. After a series of mergers and acquisitions, the corporation shifted from a washing-machine manufacturer to a manufacturer of a full line of home appliances. Recently it has broadened its mis-

[4] Booz-Allen & Hamilton, "Management of New Products," 1968.

[5] Adapted from Parker M. Holmes, Ralph E. Brownlee, and Robert Bartels, eds., *Readings in Marketing* (Columbus, Ohio: Charles E. Merrill Books, Inc., 1963), pp. 316–19.

sion to include "life support" products. The term "life support," first used to describe systems designed to maintain a habitable environment for astronauts in space, has been broadened in concept to describe appliances serving man in his home. The concept of life support leads away from washing machines toward such products as central air conditioners, central vacuum cleaners and dehumidifiers, and toward total environmental control. The evolution from a company making wooden iceboxes to one defining its mission as the business of life support is evidence of a profound change in an organization. Research, engineering, development, and marketing forces have to be organized differently to meet the challenges of such a broad concept of business.

Knowledge of the mortality of new product ideas can be very useful in helping to examine the cost- and revenue-generating activities entailed in new product selection and development. This is demonstrated in Fig. 6–5.

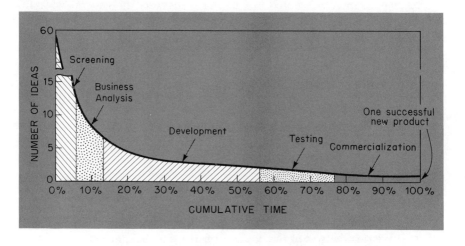

**FIG. 6-5 Mortality of New Product Ideas (by Stage of Evolution—
51 Companies)**

Source: Management Research Department, Booz-Allen & Hamilton Inc.

1. *Search:* Studies designed to locate potential additions to a firm's product line or capabilities. Market studies, research and development work, and acquisition studies all qualify as part of a well-organized search program. (This phase is not shown in Figure 6–5.)
2. *Screening:* Rapid, low-cost studies which eliminate weak proposals and informally weigh the relative desirability of promising proposals.
3. *Business analysis:* Careful, detailed studies to clarify, improve, and appraise the proposals that survive preliminary analyses. The end result of this activity is a recommendation to scrap

the proposal, defer action, or proceed to develop a tangible product or capability.

4. *Development:* The transformation of the proposal into a tangible product and process results in a working model.
5. *Product Testing:* In this stage market tests to measure the reactions of resellers and final buyers to the product are conducted.
6. *Commercialization:* Involvement in full-scale production and marketing operations to establish the product in its desired place in the firm's product line results.

Even though one new product idea in sixty passes all five stages and reaches introduction, the mortality rate is still high, although it is better than it was ten years ago (primarily because of better opportunity assessment). It is estimated that almost 40 percent of new products are failures, as indicated by Table 6–2. A slightly more optimistic estimate is given by the National Industrial Conference Board,[6] which found that one out of every three products put on the market failed. Despite the failure figure, most good marketers consider the risk of not developing new products to be considerably greater than the risk of product failures.

TABLE 6-2 Rate of Commercial Success

	New Product Ideas	Projects Development Product	New Products Introduced
		Success Percentages	
All Industry Groups	1.7%	14.5%	62.5%
Chemical	2%	18%	59%
Consumer Packaged Goods	2%	11%	63%
Electrical Machinery	1%	13%	63%
Metal Fabricators	3%	11%	71%
Non-Electrical Machinery	2%	21%	59%
Raw Material Processors	5%	14%	59%

Source: Management Research Department, Booz-Allen & Hamilton Inc.

PACKAGING

In keeping with the "total product" concept, the marketing or product manager must also give serious consideration to the packaging of his

---

[6] Reported in William V. Muse and Robert J. Kegerreis, "Technological Innovation and Marketing Management: Implications for Corporate Policy," *Journal of Marketing,* xxxiii, No. 4 (October 1969), 3.

firm's products. To enjoy a sales boost a product need not necessarily be physically new. Anything which makes it new in the eyes of current or new target customers makes it an essentially new product for marketing planning purposes. In many cases a new package for an existing product has been a major factor in a marketing strategy. For example, aerosol cans made virtually new products out of shaving cream, whipped topping, cheese spread, and many other products which had been around a long time. Other illustrations of new packaging are the six-packs, eight-packs, flip top cans, wide mouth bottles, and all the various sizes and shapes of beverage containers now on the market.

In 1966, U.S. manufacturers invested $15 billion for packaging material and $11 billion more for equipment and services,[7] which is almost twice the amount spent on advertising. One reason for the magnitude of this expenditure, other than for shipping and container purposes, is that packaging is an efficient point-of-purchase means of product differentiation and advertising.

Today's mushrooming of self-service retail outlets will continue to make packaging an extremely important feature of a product. In the absence of a sales clerk, a package must catch the customer's eye, show him what the product does, and then sell it to him. This is no easy task, and those who can do it best at the least cost will enjoy success in the self-service age.

Recently, another dimension has been added to the packaging problem. The realization of the consequences of continued pollution of the physical environment has led to increased pressure upon business to play a more active role in pollution control. The challenge to the firm is for a package which not only performs all the functions cited above, but which also will not become a pollutant when disposed. Environmental constraints will take on increased emphasis in the 1970s as effective means are sought to control pollution.

SERVICE

One factor, all too often overlooked, is the role of service in the marketing program. In today's age of consumerism, service in all forms, especially post-purchase service, is critical. Because the modern consumer is infinitely more sophisticated than his predecessor, and because of the current levels of price, quality, and advertising competition, customer service provides an excellent basis upon which to compete.

Inadequate service practices are sources of complaint for consumers and such business critics as Ralph Nader and Vance Packard. Responsible management and product policy in line with consumer interest can go a long way toward preventing future government intervention in the business sphere as well as undesirable and damaging publicity. The need for socially responsible behavior has always been present. However, some businesses have been slow to adopt the idea that service has social dimen-

---

[7] Dik Warren Twedt, "How Much Value Can Be Added Through Packaging?" *Journal of Marketing*, xxxii, No. 1 (January 1968), 58.

sions and that obligations to customers do not necessarily end with the sale. The auto industry is an example of the governmental concern and public disfavor which result from an industry's failure to recognize the importance of social considerations.

The modern concept is that the seller's obligations extend to seeing that the customer receives satisfaction in the use of the product. Only at this point can the transaction be considered complete. Although this idea is coming to be accepted more frequently by business, it is still often a forced acceptance. Business faces the increasing possibility of having customer satisfaction forced upon it in forms less desirable than those to which an initially mature and responsible attitude would have led. The lesson is clear; one hopes that future generations of managers can learn and profit from it.

IBM is an example of a company that uses service as one of the most important aspects of its marketing program. It emphasizes the marketing of a total package of computer services, including maintenance of the system, by providing systems engineers, programming consultants, and computer operators.

Pricing Policy

UNDERLYING CONSIDERATIONS

Prices and pricing policies represent probably the most troublesome area of marketing management. It is said that people will buy anything if the price is right. But arriving at that exact price and doing so in advance of one's competition is an infinitely complex procedure. The rewards for selecting wisely are sales, profits, and an advantageous market position.

Prices are monetary manifestations or expressions of value, and as such they act as regulators of the economy. Prices are, therefore, of central interest to economists, governments, consumers, and businessmen. Government officials and economists are concerned with prices and price levels as a measure or pulse of the economy as a whole. Consumers are interested in prices because, in conjunction with income, they determine the possibilities for acquiring ownership or use of products and services. Prices are important to the businessman because they shape his profit picture by indicating the margin between revenues and operating costs.

As indicated, virtually everyone has a vested interest in prices. Although many different executives are concerned with pricing, it is top management that determines price policy after consideration of various price determinants and restraints.

PRICE DETERMINANTS

There is no simple formula for management to use when making pricing decisions, because many interacting factors require consideration, and their importance varies with each pricing problem. Some critical factors that must be considered are:

The Economic Framework in Which the Firm Operates. For purposes of analysis, economists classify the situations in which a firm operates as pure competition, monopolistic competition, oligopoly, and monopoly.[8]

Customer Demand. In demand analysis, management tries to establish the volume of products that can be sold within a price schedule during a specific period of time. Concepts of inelasticity, elasticity, and cross-elasticity of demand are often utilized in pricing decisions. In addition, the appraisal of demand must examine consumer preferences. Consumer response to prices is affected by psychological and other cultural considerations as well as economics.

Costs. Cost factors usually set the lower limit on pricing. Several cost concepts are useful in price determination. Full or incremental cost analysis and break-even analysis are examples.

Competition. Whenever a firm makes a price decision, it must anticipate action by its competitors. Competitive pricing action, or the possibility of such action, sets an upper limit on prices and therefore concerns pricing managers.

Company Objectives. The company's objectives reflect and influence price policy. For instance, a company may choose to be a style or quality leader, which would be reflected in the price policy. Maintenance of marketing share and promotion policy may also influence a company's pricing decisions.

RESTRAINTS ON PRICING DECISIONS

Legal Considerations. The law regulating pricing decisions is complex. Large firms consider the law and the economics of the situation, and the probable reaction of government agencies and the courts in reaching many pricing decisions.

Technology. Keen competition created when a number of firms duplicate research efforts frequently results in overcapacity. This equilibrating of technology, accompanied by shorter periods of exclusivity, often leads to aggressive price competition.

[8] These models and other economic considerations are treated in the following books: Kristian S. Palda, *Economic Analysis for Marketing Decisions* (Englewood Cliffs, N.J.: Prentice-Hall, Inc., 1969); George J. Stigler, *The Theory of Price*, rev. ed. (New York: The Macmillan Company, 1952); Milton H. Spencer and Louis Siegelman, *Managerial Economics* (Homewood, Ill.: Richard D. Irwin, Inc., 1964); Joel Dean, *Managerial Economics* (Englewood Cliffs, N.J.: Prentice-Hall, Inc., 1951); Edward H. Chamberlin, *The Theory of Monopolistic Competition*, 6th ed. (Cambridge, Mass.: Harvard University Press, 1948); Alfred Oxenfeldt, David Miller, Abraham Schuchman, and Charles Winick, *Insights into Pricing* (Belmont, Cal.: Wadsworth Publishing Co., 1961); Alfred R. Oxenfeldt, *Pricing for Marketing Executives* (Belmont, Cal.: Wadsworth Publishing Co., 1961).

Social Implications. This is perhaps an even more rapidly expanding source of pricing restraints than technology. Ethics, social responsibility, and consumerism are elements in price setting today.

Price competition is also often closely scrutinized by government agencies for the protection of the small businessman. Retailers in low-income areas are under considerable pressure to keep quality up and prices down. Businesses, both large and small, must do their share in helping keep inflation under control, which entails sound, responsible pricing policies.

THE PRICING TASK OF MARKETING MANAGEMENT

Marketing management must be cognizant of the above factors, particularly the competitive pressures on pricing. For the marketing manager, however, the most controllable elements are usually marketing costs. Marketing management must concern itself with evaluation of the demand for a product and determination of the least costly, most effective marketing mix to stimulate profitable demand for that product.

The problem of determining value is difficult and subjective, particularly for new products. With all products, the price determines the amount sold and plays a significant role in establishing the profit or loss on a transaction. If the price is set too high, it is possible that insufficient units will be sold to permit the firm's recovery of initial expenses incurred in product development. On the other hand, if the price is too low, the firm might not be able to cover all its marginal costs.

One reason that price setting is so complicated is that cost analysis is extremely difficult. According to Joel Dean, a successful price policy for a new product should achieve three objectives—getting the product accepted, maintaining the market in the face of growing competition, and producing profits.[9]

Before decisions on objectives can be made, it is necessary to study the actual and potential demand for the product, ascertain the costs of manufacturing and selling it at various demand levels, establish market targets, develop communications strategy, and select the channel of distribution. Costs are usually easier to estimate than demand. Demand estimation involves analysis of the potential for the new product in terms of all the available substitutes for it. The question of substitute competition is difficult and complicates the demand estimates.

PRICE DETERMINATION APPROACHES

Kotler describes the following three approaches to pricing a firm's products—cost-oriented, demand-oriented and competition-oriented.[10]

[9] Joel Dean, "Pricing a New Product," *The Controller* (April 1955), pp. 163–65.

[10] Philip Kotler, *Marketing Management, Analysis, Planning, and Control* (Englewood Cliffs, N.J.: Prentice-Hall, Inc., 1967), pp. 360–69.

Cost-oriented pricing is usually manifested in one of three ways. The first is simply to attach a fixed percentage of cost to an item in an *ad valorem* fashion. Small retailers normally employ this method, which, in most cases, is quite simple to compute as costing is no particular problem. For example, if a gross of candy bars costs $7.20, then the candy bars are 5¢ each. A variety store owner might then sell them for 10¢ or 100 percent markup while the drugstore may charge only 8¢ or 60 percent markup. Generally the markups will vary from item to item and from one point in time to another for the same item.

A cost-plus pricing arrangement is a second method used in cases where costs are not readily predictable. Under cost-plus pricing the buyer will repay all costs to the vendor plus a predetermined percentage over costs as remuneration or profit margin. For example, if an item costs $.50 and a 10% profit margin is required, the item would be priced at $.55.

A third cost-oriented approach is target pricing. In this case target refers to a desired rate of return based on a prior estimation of demand expressed in units. With an available estimate for demand, costs can be computed and a price can be attached to the units to yield the desired target return. This method is most common in heavy manufacturing concerns.

Demand-oriented. The intensity of consumer demand rather than total unit costs is the focal point of demand-oriented pricing. Higher demand results in a higher price. Costs, as long as they are covered, are ignored.

There are a number of very important factors which can alter the demand schedule for a product. Some of these are:

1. availability of substitutes
2. ease of want satisfaction
3. durability
4. urgency of need
5. impact of total price
6. income
7. promotion
8. population
9. competitive pressures.

Generally the demand schedule will be altered by changes in any of these nine elements. Consequently, more effort is often spent in obtaining information about these elements than in developing the traditional economic-type demand curves.

Competition-oriented Pricing. This is probably the easiest, though not necessarily the best method to price products. Many firms employing this method will not match competitors exactly, but rather will try to maintain a certain percentage above or below the going rate depending on conditions. Here no fixed relationship exists between price, costs, or demand and, since in many cases these are extremely elusive figures anyway, it is a logical assumption on the part of a firm that the average price level will approximate a reasonable margin.

The effects of pure price competition are sorely felt by many companies. When the marketing manager chooses to lower his price he realizes that his competition can immediately do the same. Gas wars are typical results of this competition. If carried to the limit, the weak businesses usually fold and stronger organizations may suffer short-term effects. Price cuts are generally the best strategy only if (1) competitor's prices must be met, or (2) the price cut is the result of product or process changes.

PRICING NEW PRODUCTS

The best starting point in determining a price policy for new products is to choose one or variations of one or more of the following objectives: [11]

1. market skimming
2. market penetration
3. return on investment
4. promotion of the product line
5. ethical pricing or "satisficing."

A skimming policy is aimed at those persons who desire and can afford the product despite an initially high price, which is set in order to maximize profits in the short run. As purchases by market innovators decrease, the price is lowered to attract the later adopters of new products. An example of this process is the history of color television pricing. A policy of this nature is usually used when no immediate competition is anticipated.

On the other hand, penetration-pricing policies seek to maximize sales volume at a satisfactory level of profits. Thus, a lower price is used initially in order to help the firm penetrate certain markets, develop brand loyalty, stymie would-be competitors, and thereby generate more stable long-run profitability. Ford Motor Company successfully accomplished this objective in pricing the Maverick.

Return on investment pricing requires more quantitative manipulations in that potential returns available at different prices and estimated sales volumes must be calculated. That price which most nearly yields the desired rate of return on investment is then selected. Airline manufacturers often use this pricing strategy.

A full product line can be offered with the strategy that sales of one product will lead to complementary sales of others; this is a "full-line" pricing policy. This may entail pricing some products at relatively low prices and others at relatively high prices. Probably the ultimate in this strategy is Gillette's pricing of razors for use with its blades. The razor may be priced from zero to two dollars, depending on market objectives.

An ethical pricing policy evolves from an overriding concern for public

[11] See Joel Dean, "Pricing a New Product," *The Controller* (April 1955), pp. 163–65.

welfare. This would occur, for example, in combating inflation or for public health reasons. Good examples include the U.S. Steel decision to hold prices down at the request of President Kennedy during the 1963 recession, or the Upjohn Pharmaceutical Company's decision to price a new cancer inhibitor at a price considerably less than necessary to recover production and development costs.

Product, package, service, and price are only a few of the elements characterizing a firm's total "offer" to the consumer. Clearly these elements are related to each other and to other elements not yet considered, such as available promotion and distribution resources. All of these elements of the mix must be in harmony with one another if a company is to survive and grow. Additional elements of promotion and distribution are discussed in Chapter 7.

7

PROMOTION AND
DISTRIBUTION POLICIES

When the needs and wants of customers and potential customers have been identified and analyzed, and a research-based product development program has been implemented, a most important, difficult, and creative marketing task must be initiated. Consumers must be informed about the firm's goods and services, they must have access to the firm's offerings, and they must be motivated to buy. These are fundamental activities in the study and operation of marketing.

Promotion Policy

MARKETING COMMUNICATIONS

Information can be considered a most valuable resource in today's advanced societies. It stimulates almost all economic activity and growth. Quality, not quantity, determines the value of information and distinguishes good marketing communicators from bad. With an estimated $18 billion expenditure for advertising in 1968 [1] and $45 billion [2] for personal selling, the American market is saturated with commercial information.

Theodore Levitt captured the enormous impact of advertising when he wrote, "Wherever we turn, advertising will be forcibly thrust on us in an intrusive orgy of abrasive sound and sight, all to induce us to do something we might not ordinarily do, or to induce us to do it differently. This massive and persistent effort crams increasingly more commercial noise into the same, few, strained 24 hours of the day." [3] Thus, each day the

[1] *Marketing/Communications*, No. 297 (August 1969), 69.

[2] G. David Hughes, "A New Tool for Sales Managers," *Journal of Marketing Research*, i (May 1964), 32.

[3] Theodore Levitt, "The Morality (?) of Advertising," *Harvard Business Review*, xlviii, No. 4 (July–August 1970), 84.

average family of four is exposed to more than 1,500 separate advertising messages, almost two per minute.[4]

As a complex process, advertising and other forms of promotion have impact, not only directly on the receiver, but also indirectly through a "group of socially related and influenced individuals whose attitudes and actions are affected by these relationships."[5] Therefore, the quality of communication is often determined by how well it fits into the social system and stimulates sales. A basic understanding of the communication process is desirable for insight into the role of promotion in marketing and society.

THE COMMUNICATION PROCESS

Broadly speaking, there are three necessary ingredients for communication to take place: a source, a message, and a receiver.[6] Market communications (messages) flow between the firm (source) and four main groups of receivers. These are (1) consumers; (2) various sales-supporting personnel such as wholesalers, retailers, and other middlemen in the system; (3) other members of distribution channels and the marketing system not directly under the control of the firm, such as advertising agencies; and finally (4) material and resource suppliers such as financial and governmental agencies.

It is desirable for each element in the flow of messages to act as both source and receiver so that a return flow of communications, called feedback, is accomplished. Feedback must be present for any meaningful analysis of market communication and its effectiveness. Figure 7–1 illustrates this circular flow of communication or messages.

MARKETING COMMUNICATIONS ANALYSIS

Business is separated from its customers in several ways: distance, time, socioeconomic gaps, information, and interests. The promotional efforts of firms attempt to bridge these gaps. Business information about products and services reaches the consumer through advertising, personal selling, and sales promotional channels.

Figure 7–2 illustrates a conceptual framework for analyzing marketing communications, based on a concept originally developed by scientists studying communications theory in electrical engineering. The upper section illustrates the classic general communications model. The source, or communicator, who could be a marketing manager, parent, salesman, or

[4] David A. Schwartz, "Measuring the Effectiveness of Your Company's Advertising," *Journal of Marketing*, xxxiii, No. 2 (April 1969), 20.

[5] M. Dale Beckman, "Are Your Messages Getting Through?" *Journal of Marketing*, xxxi, No. 3 (July 1967), 35.

[6] Edgar Crane, *Marketing Communications* (New York: John Wiley & Sons, Inc., 1965).

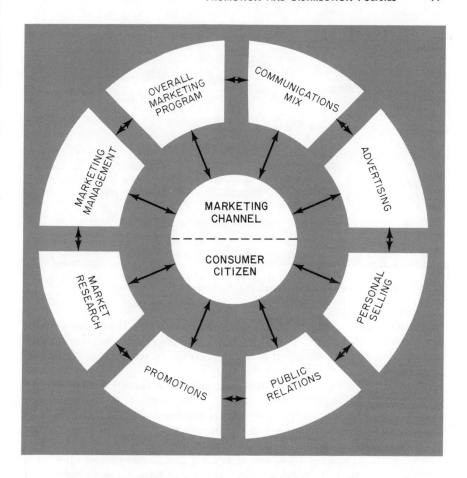

FIG. 7-1 The Communications Mix and Message Flows in an
Integrated Marketing Program

teacher, selects the information to be communicated from an infinite spectrum of messages. The message he chooses is presumably related to his objectives and is influenced by the results he hopes to obtain. Messages are transmitted through channels; they are distorted, however, by outside interference, called noise. The message, or version of it that is received, may or may not influence the recipient.

The marketing communication model shown on the bottom half of Fig. 7-2 is the classic model. Management has established its objectives and has selected the ideas or messages that must be communicated to achieve these objectives. The next task is the media selection through which the information is to be sent or transmitted—advertising, personal selling, or a personal letter, for example. Typically, it will involve a combination of media. Management anticipates that promotional messages are sent to

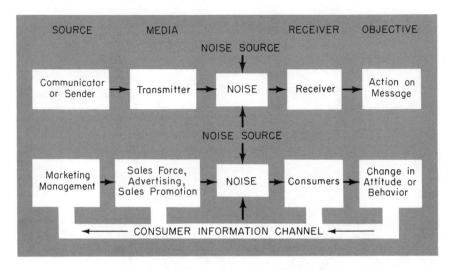

FIG. 7-2 Framework for Analyzing Marketing Communications

recipients who are under a barrage of similar messages from competition. The design is that some of the messages sent will reach receivers or consumers who will be persuaded to act in accordance with the objectives of the sender.

An open communications system has two-way channels so that the receiver can question or communicate with the sender. A communicator usually attempts to provide two-way communication by using various methods of feedback. The feedback principle is an effort to recover part of the useful output of a system in order to further control and direct it. The ultimate in market feedback is knowledge of completed sales as a result of messages. Feedback information obtained through sales and marketing research is utilized by management to assist in the appraisal of the results of the transmitted messages in order to guide product and sales strategy and to revise communication content, form, and channels.

The mass media of radio, television, and newspapers are inherently capable of conveying one-way information from the marketing organization to the intended recipients of the message; they have no provision for obtaining direct feedback. Various devices, including listenership surveys and coupon campaigns, may be used to introduce the element of two-way information flow into these one-way channels, but the vast majority of commercial media channels are not really capable of conveying a return flow of information from the market. One of the great advantages of personal selling is that it is inherently a two-way channel which permits the sender to alter or reinforce the message immediately when he perceives that the receiver does not understand or is not responding as desired. A good salesman, by watching recipient behavior, can change his presentation and his communications symbols to match the perception patterns of the receiver, thus increasing the effectiveness of the communication.

NATURE OF THE SELLING PROCESS

A sale occurs when a buyer and seller exchange title to economic goods—at retail, wholesale, and manufacturing levels, or wherever a market exists. It can occur in homes, factories, over the telephone, at an auction, or wherever a buyer and seller can communicate. The selling process can be divided into presale, selling, and postsale activities, each of which involves different communications problems. Preselling communications may be concerned with establishing a favorable image of a firm, product line, or industry. Selling activities are those that result, or are intended to result, in the completion of an economic transaction. Postsale activities include service and follow-up activities necessary to satisfy the consumer. Under the marketing concept of selling, the sale is not considered complete until the customer is convinced of the want-satisfying characteristics of the product, title has been transferred, and the customer has been satisfied.

The seller can use a variety of methods to accomplish sales and marketing objectives. The main forms are personal salesmanship, advertising, and sales promotion. Larger sellers use the three selling methods in a combination, or promotional mix, of selling effort.[7] Advertising and sales promotions are forms of mass selling. Sales promotion and merchandising activities include publicity, trade shows, conventions, exhibitions, dealer aids, and other devices. Personal selling is usually individualized selling, although selling to groups and buying committees is growing more common. One distinction frequently made between advertising and salesmanship is that salesmanship is personal and advertising is impersonal because it is transmitted through mass media. However, the objective of advertisers is to personalize their written communications to the greatest possible degree even though the sales messages cannot be tailored individually to each recipient.

Larger firms supplement their advertising and selling efforts with organized public relations and publicity programs. Publicity efforts are made to secure favorable mention in communications media about the company or products. Publicity is delivered to the readers without payment by the sponsor and appears as part of the news or entertainment content of the media. Advertising is distinguished from publicity in that advertising is purchased and paid for by the firm.

Promotion management is complicated by both the heterogeneous nature of markets and consumers and the high degree of substitutability of mix elements. For this reason, behavioral science theories are becoming increasingly useful in developing communications programs. For example, the task of the marketing economist is to describe the structure and eco-

---

[7] The "demonstration effect," a phrase coined by James S. Dusenberry, illustrates one of the significant cultural factors of marketing. Through marketing and its various institutions and agencies, such as retail stores and advertising agencies, the affluence of a productive society is demonstrated and consumption expenditures are increased by consumer contact with superior goods.

nomic actions of the market; the marketing psychologist attempts to explain the motivation and psychological reasons for consumer and market behavior. Communications programs must be built on knowledge of the basic needs of individuals, learning theory, self-image, ego involvement, brand image, risk perception, attitudes, and other socio-psychological tools.

TOTAL EFFECT

The modern trend in marketing is to begin with the desired image of a product and then to work backward to create the unique combinations of promotion media and messages to yield that image.[8] In this way, the total campaign is developed to produce one unified effect. When this campaign unity is achieved, the coordinated and interdependent media should have more impact on the buyer than would be the case if each medium carried an independent message. This approach results in campaigns better targeted to audience images, consumer-citizen activities, and is more congruent with segmentation strategies. Marshall McLuhan insightfully articulated this concept with regard to advertising.

> The continuous pressure is to create ads [campaigns] more and more in the image of audience motives and desires. The product matters less as the audience participation increases. . . . The need is to make the ad include the audience experience. . . . The steady trend in advertising is to manifest the product as an integral part of large social purposes and processes. With very large budgets the commercial artists have tended to develop the ad into an icon, and icons are not specialist fragments or aspects but unified and compressed images of complex kind. They focus a large region of experience in tiny compass.[9]

The combination of proper salesmanship, journal advertising, direct mail, public relations, and all other customer-impinging messages should provide the customer with a feeling of consuming the product before consumption. If properly actualized, the consumer feels little or no risk because the product is visualized not as an object but as part of the living process.[10] As Levitt said, "The purpose of the product is not what the engineer explicitly says it is, but what the consumer implicitly demands that it shall be. Thus, the consumer consumes not things, but expected benefits—not cosmetics but the satisfactions of the allurements they promise; not quarter inch drills, but quarter inch holes; not stock in companies, but

---

[8] Gilbert Harrell, "Definition of Company Mission, Goals, Objectives, Strategy and Tactics," unpublished manuscript, The Pennsylvania State University, July 1970.

[9] Marshall McLuhan, *Understanding Media* (New York: New American Library, 1964), p. 201.

[10] See Donald Cox, "Risk Perception and Information Handling in Consumer Behavior," Division of Research, Harvard University, 1967.

capital gains. . . ." [11] The total-effect concept of promotion provides the approach to promotion coordination that is necessary if the full impact of promotion expenditures is to reach and motivate the greatest possible number of customers.

PROMOTION OBJECTIVES

The starting point in communications planning is similar to that in other marketing planning tasks—establish objectives and targets and devise the right combination of programs and techniques to achieve those targets. Historically, advertising and personal selling were treated as independent functions. They are still so organized in many firms, although the trend is to place these functions under one marketing executive. Executives concerned with a total view of the promotion-marketing task try to develop a program that is soundly based in terms of knowledge of consumer problems, attitudes, and desires as they relate to the products being promoted. Questions asked by a marketing manager about advertising or about a particular piece of copy include:

> What is the purpose of the advertising?
> Is it designed to develop good will, influence dealers, or accomplish any of a variety of objectives?
> Is the advertising focused on the needs of the target markets and on the specific types of consumers being solicited?

A professional salesman calling on a customer or prospect usually has specific objectives he wishes to achieve in each interview. In some cases he hopes to introduce himself to the buyer or demonstrate the product; in others he hopes to close the sale. Still other interviews may be follow-up calls to handle service questions and problems or to obtain leads for future business. Advertisements and advertising programs also involve specific objectives. The objectives determine many of the details of the program, including copy, media, budget, and evaluation. It is not readily possible to determine just by looking at an advertisement whether it is, or will be, effective. Its effectiveness must be evaluated in terms of its successful achievement of specific objectives. These objectives include:

> Making an immediate sale
> Building primary demand
> Introducing a price deal
> Informing about a product's availability
> Building brand recognition, preference, or insistence
> Informing about a new product's availability, features, or price
> Aiding salesmen by building retailer awareness of a product
> Creating a reputation for service, reliability, or research strength
> Increasing market share
> Modifying existing product appeals and buying motives

[11] Levitt, *op. cit.*, p. 91.

Informing about new uses for a product
Increasing the number or quality of retail outlets
Building the over-all company image
Reaching new areas or new segments of population within existing
areas

Analysis of a marketing situation suggests the extent to which these objectives can be achieved by advertising, personal selling, or sales promotion. In general, advertising expands the base of consumer demand for a product and undertakes the additional promotional efforts required to sell it. Personal selling is usually emphasized in such fields as insurance and investment selling, where the product involves service and specialized knowledge; where the product is complex, such as in industrial marketing; or where a significant amount of money is involved, as in the selling of automobiles and real estate. In the case of convenience goods, such as foods, the selling effort supplementing advertising is sales promotional in nature. For foods and tobacco, advertising is usually the major part of the promotional mix. Personal sales efforts are used to acquire retailers, to insure that products have a favorable shelf position, and for similar purposes.

Within the framework of the entire promotional campaign there may be several people or groups of people with their own sets of objectives. For example, on a call to one customer a salesman may merely wish to obtain an introduction to a potential buyer, while on another he may fully intend to finalize a sale. At the same time, an advertising manager may be pouring over pieces of copy for an upcoming campaign trying to determine how he can most effectively inform the greatest number of potential customers at the least cost. However, if one takes a more detailed view of the promotional program it is possible to differentiate three major objectives: [12] (1) Stimulate product awareness, in the hope that it will combine with various inputs from the marketing strategy adopted and eventually culminate in a sale; (2) trigger a sale in a buyer who has already decided to purchase and who is engaged in a search for the right product; and (3) maintain the interests and patronage of regular buyers. Competitors will continually attempt to sell customers, and wise marketing managers will recognize the importance of retaining the patronage of past customers. Analysis of specific marketing situations can help to indicate the extent to which each of these objectives can be achieved by the various combinations of personal selling, advertising, sales promotion, and publicity.

PERSONAL SELLING

Personal selling expenses are the largest single marketing cost for many firms. The management of personal selling, therefore, becomes a most important marketing management area from the viewpoint of cost as well

[12] James F. Engel, Hugh G. Wales, and Martin R. Warshaw, *Promotional Strategy* (Homewood, Ill.: Richard D. Irwin & Sons, Inc., 1967), pp. 98–99.

as revenue. The tasks of sales managers can be divided into two main areas: (1) sales force management and (2) sales administration. Sales force management duties are those traditionally delegated to the sales manager. Sales administration duties represent those added by marketing concept changes.[13] The following list details the sales manager's duties in each area:

Sales Force Management

Recruiting: Finding and hiring suitable candidates for selling positions, determined by sales objectives, job analysis, and manpower needs.

Selection: Hiring those applicants who, through testing, seem most likely to become effective salesmen.

Training: Instructing new salesmen and "refreshing" experienced salesmen about current products and developments.

Motivation: Showing salesmen how financial, professional, and personal goals are achieved by working to attain company goals.

Stimulation: Providing tangible motivation tactics, such as contests and conventions, and integrating all aspects of an effective sales force management program.

Supervision: Insuring that salesmen follow company policies and regulations in attaining specific sales goals.

Compensation: Combining motivation, stimulation, control, and direction into a monetary plan ranging from straight commission through salary and commission to straight salary.

Goals: Effective personal leadership; achieving sales targets.

Sales Administration

Planning: Integrating individual and corporate selling efforts with other marketing mix elements of the firm, as indicated by market research; planning innovation in products and processes.

Determination of Potential: Forecasting, through a quantitative estimate reflecting qualitative factors, the sales expected in a period by following a given marketing plan. This figure is basic to all planning.

Organization and Coordination: Integrating selling efforts and relations with the marketing and other departments of the firm to achieve established goals; establishing and maintaining two-way communication.

Audit and Control: Reviewing and measuring sales activities as to both sales and profit goal attainment.

Innovation and Selling: Adapting to ever-changing customer needs and market opportunity by improving selling processes.

Goals: Establishing and maintaining the desired public and competitive image; ensuring market share; integrating with other elements of marketing mix.

The new salesman is visualized as a "problem-solver," an educator, and an empathizer.[14] His new role extends beyond strategies and profits to a

[13] Eugene J. Kelley and William Lazer, "Basic Duties of the Modern Sales Department," *Industrial Marketing*, xlv (April 1960), 68.

[14] Leslie M. Dawson, "Toward a New Concept of Sales Management," *Journal of Marketing*, xxxiv, No. 2 (April 1970), 33–38.

total involvement in the marketing process. Progressive sales force management and administration involve total human resource development, through emphasis on personal fulfillment and contribution. The new salesman is seen as a territory manager who utilizes a full range of marketing tools. The importance of selling and a good salesman becomes apparent when one recognizes that many companies have picked their leading executives from the ranks of sales personnel.

ADVERTISING

The role played by advertising in the marketing programs of individual firms varies among industries and from firm to firm. Some advertising is concerned with direct selling—for example, that of correspondence schools or mail-order houses. But the objective of most advertising is to present information about a product, arouse interest, build desire, and get consumers in a favorable frame of mind to try the product. The product itself will actually be sold by a salesman in direct contact with the prospect. Or the product may be promoted through advertising and sold in a self-service store, aided by store displays and promotion. Advertising is more than salesmanship in print. The specific tasks assigned to advertising will depend on the marketing objectives to be achieved, the other elements of the communications mix, the products sold, consumer buying habits, and distribution patterns.

Advertising has two main aspects. The first concerns the creative part of composing advertisements—selecting appeals, writing copy, and what is termed the "art" of advertising. The other aspect of advertising is concerned with such problems as measuring the effectiveness of advertisements and studying the allocation of dollars to the various advertising and promotional alternatives available. This is the management side of advertising.

Advertising and selling will be fundamentally altered in the coming years in response to the view of the firm as an integrated technological and marketing system focusing on the profitable satisfaction of consumption needs. The role of business advertising and marketing management in the 1970s will include the following changes—many of which are already well under way:

- Greater emphasis on marketing planning and sophisticated market research leading to the development of on-line marketing information systems—so that marketing and advertising can be supported by an integrated company-wide market-oriented effort.
- More environmental sensitivity in both domestic and international markets with more communication channels and an increased ability to translate new customer needs into profitable action programs. The advertising executive and the salesman must become environmentalists in order to manage information.
- More attention to advertising and promotion aimed at market enlargement rather than market maintenance.

- More concern with and research on the specific information needs of decision-makers and customers.
- Demand, fostered by progress in management science and information technology, for more precision, speed, and quality of decision-making and analysis.

As a result of these developments the posture of the professional advertising manager and marketing manager is changing. A few of his new roles are:

- As a key corporate marketing and communications executive who will utilize a full range of decision-making tools in his operations.
- As a market information officer who will develop objective information that will be utilized in corporate level policy decisions which will modify the customer's benefit-price-risk ratio.
- As an important component of the product and services mix itself, the advertiser and sales manager perform vital information services for customers.
- As a corporate officer who will help in the redefinition of the role and responsibilities of business in a transitional world society characterized by changes in values, norms, institutions, and in individual and business attitudes.

These new challenges do not diminish the importance of traditional concepts of advertising and salesmanship. However, new dimensions are being added, changing the role of the advertising and sales executive to one encompassing a larger sphere of responsibility. An indication of this trend is the addition of managerial duties that involve the advertising and promotion functions covering market engineering, communication, and development. It is here that the new marketing technology (outlined in Chapter 2) is on its way to revolutionizing advertising and sales management. The basis of successful business promotion will continue to be creative programs based on understanding the customer and his changing problems. Marketing strategy developed in response to changing consumer requirements and expectations is a major step in contending with future marketing situations.

PROMOTION EVALUATION

Advertising, selling, and sales promotion are areas of business decision-making where quality and effectiveness are difficult to evaluate. However, an Association of National Advertisers poll revealed that 80 percent of its members felt that the effectiveness of advertising could be measured.[15]

Charles Ramond [16] has classified advertising research according to the type of decision that is to be made:

[15] Association of National Advertisers, "Probing Ad Effectiveness," *Printer's Ink* (May 8, 1964), 43–44.

[16] Charles K. Ramond, "New Developments in U.S. Advertising Research," an Address to the Institute de Recherche et d'Etudes Publications, Paris, May 7, 1968.

Decision	Type of Research
What to say	Theme or Concept Research
How to say it	Copy Research
Where, when, and how often to say it	Media Research
How much to spend	Sales Research

In *theme* research, brand managers are attempting to match product characteristics with desired images. They are more interested in what they want customers to know and believe than in what should be "said." *Copy* research is used to test the words, illustrations, and design aspects of ads to determine if they convey the desired message. In *media* research the manager is interested in determining the exposure to various stimuli from magazines, television shows, radio programs, newspapers, and other media. Sales research is designed to measure the total effects of advertising budgets in terms of communication messages and sales effects.

The measurement of selling effectiveness is complicated because of territorial differences such as population density, ease of travel, and geographical usefulness of the product. The initial step is to evaluate the total sales potential for each territory; the salesman's efforts reflecting his profit contribution as well as sales volume, are evaluated against the findings of this initial research. Because there often are variations in competition from region to region, competitive dynamics should also be considered. One means of accomplishing this is to break down elements such as purchases by new and old customers, size of individual orders, number of service calls and selling calls, and to utilize these variables to pinpoint problems and opportunities.

The importance of proper evaluation in advertising and selling can not be overemphasized. A case in point is a company that had not evaluated a promotion campaign for a sophisticated drug product for three years. The anticipated introduction of a new entry in the same drug class and an awareness that the older product was not satisfactorily holding its share of the market led to a marketing study of physicians. During the course of the interviews it became clear that physicians did not understand the terminology used by the company's advertising and sales people. In tracing the source of several abbreviations for technical medical terms used extensively by the company, it was found that the terms originated at the home office of the company and not in medical schools or in medical practice, as company personnel believed. Further investigation showed that several million dollars had been spent in delivering technical messages that could not be decoded in the marketplace.

Distribution Policy

Whereas traditional marketing thought dwells on the generation of demand for goods and services, and on the motivation of consumers to purchase, these are only a part of the "marketing equation." It goes without saying that stimulation of the consumer purchase mechanism would be fruitless unless there exists, in the marketplace, an available supply of goods and services. The generation of this availability by the facilitating of a constant flow of goods and services through market channels is the responsibility of the physical distribution element of the marketing mix. Thus, the perennial problem of those directly concerned with physical distribution is the optimization of time and place utility for marketable goods and services, while minimizing costs. The physical distribution function, often called the "gray area between manufacturing and marketing," encompasses such activities as traffic management, warehousing, order hauling, inventory control, and in-plant material handling and production control. Regarding the management of these activities, the current emphasis is on a systems approach designed to achieve a tradeoff between optimal consumer service and minimal operating costs.

Recently, numerous developments have focused greater attention on physical distribution. The advent of the computer has brought with it the capability to rapidly process vast quantities of data, facilitating not only a general systems approach to logistical problems, but also such specific quantitative techniques as linear programming transportation models. Secondly, while the over-all costs of physical distribution, such as freight rates and labor, are increasing, they represent cost factors that are more susceptible to budgetary controls and thus offer management an effective means of enhancing profitability. Third, the complex logistical systems characterizing today's market have been a byproduct of the proliferation of new products that are not only available in innumerable models and colors but also require large amounts of maintenance repair parts. Finally, recent court rulings have raised questions on the legality of certain pricing practices, such as delivered pricing, resulting in a sharper focus on transfer and other costs from a total cost perspective.[17]

The future will witness an even greater importance of the physical distribution function.[18] Not only will new and effective means of facilitating flows of goods and services within institutional channels be required, but methods of direct distribution from institutions to the ultimate consumer also will be necessary. The fulfillment of such challenges requires a sys-

[17] Edward W. Smykay, Donald J. Bowersox, and Frank H. Mossman, *Physical Distribution Management*, rev. ed. (New York: The Macmillan Company, 1968), pp. 8–15.

[18] For readers interested in a more extensive coverage of physical distribution, the following references are suggested: Helmy H. Baligh and Leon E. Richartz, *Vertical Market Structures* (Boston: Allyn and Bacon, Inc., 1967); J. L. Heskett, Robert M. Ivie, and Nicholas A. Glaskowsky, Jr., *Business Logistics* (New York: The Ronald Press Company, 1964); Donald J. Bowersox, Edward W. Smykay, and Bernard J. LaLonde, *Physical Distribution Management*, rev. ed. (New York: The Macmillan Company, 1968); Charles A. Taft, *Management of Traffic and Physical Distribution*, 4th ed. (Homewood, Ill.: Richard D. Irwin, Inc., 1968); Norton E. Marks and Robert M. Taylor, *Marketing Logistics: Perspectives and Viewpoints* (New York: John Wiley & Sons, Inc., 1967); Norman E. Daniel and J. Richard Jones, *Business Logistics* (Boston: Allyn and Bacon, Inc., 1969); John F. Magee, *Physical-Distribution Systems* (New York: McGraw-Hill Book Company, 1967).

tems approach responsive to the influence of all societal and environmental forces, not just to internal variables or factors limited to the direct sphere of operation.

DISTRIBUTION CHANNELS

The path followed by a product as it changes ownership and accumulates utilities in the movement from production to consumption is known as its channel of distribution. The dollar costs of distribution are among the highest expense areas in marketing. For example, in metals, chemicals, and petroleum they are about 25 percent of the sales dollar, and they total over 30 percent of sales in the food industries.[19] Because of high costs, a large amount of important research is being focused on cost reduction. The "forgotten frontier" of distribution lies in examining the effects of distribution on the entire marketing program, including demand stimulation and effective merchandising. Before discussing these elements, the reader should be aware of the variety of basic channel options available to marketers, as shown in Fig. 7–3.

Option 1 is direct selling. This is the shortest channel a product can follow to the market, for the maker sells the product directly to the user. This is the channel followed by a farmer selling his own eggs from a roadside stand, the Fuller Brush Company or the Realsilk Hosiery Company selling directly to consumers in their homes, and General Electric when selling a large electronics installation directly to industrial purchasers.

Option 2 represents the channel followed by the large appliance manufacturers who sell in quantity to a retailer such as a department store, discount house, or mail-order house. The retailer in turn sells to consumers. Retail institutions are the most numerous channel intermediaries. Option 3 is a channel typically followed by manufacturers of food or cigarettes, who sell to specialized wholesalers, who in turn distribute to retailers, who sell the goods to the consumer. Option 4 is an example of a channel in which the producer uses the service of an agent middleman, such as a sales agent, for the initial dispersion of goods. The agent in turn may distribute to wholesalers, who in turn sell to retailers. Other options are possible, as indicated by Option n.

In practice the exercise of channel options becomes more complicated than this sketch indicates. A manufacturer may use different channels at different times for different products in different markets. The problem of selecting the most satisfactory channel of distribution for a product is complex. Each situation has to be examined individually, and the decision must be made on the basis of external considerations, as well as the nature of the product and the position of the manufacturer and consumer. Careful analysis of a distribution channel problem includes a detailed consumer analysis in which the number, type, location, and buying habits of con-

[19] Robert P. Neuschel, "Physical Distribution—Forgotten Frontier," *Harvard Business Review*, xlv, No. 2 (March–April 1967), 125.

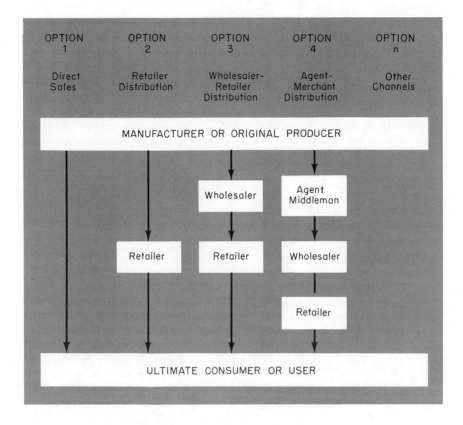

OPTION 1	OPTION 2	OPTION 3	OPTION 4	OPTION n
Direct Sales	Retailer Distribution	Wholesaler- Retailer Distribution	Agent- Merchant Distribution	Other Channels

FIG. 7-3   Channel Options for Manufactured Goods

sumers are considered. In addition, existing trade channels of competitors are scrutinized and the nature of the distribution and promotional task is assessed to see which function could best be performed by the manufacturer and which by the middleman.

Channel decisions may vary among manufacturers of like goods. A manufacturer in a strong financial position with a wide line of related products may sell directly to retailers. A manufacturer of a single product is not able to do this so easily. The unit value of a commodity is also important. Large appliances are most likely to be sold directly to the consumer than are food products. On the other hand, a large buyer, such as a chain store, is able to buy low unit value products directly from the manufacturer.

Cox, Goodman, and Fichandler [20] identify three separate kinds of flows in distribution. These are movements through geographic space, movements through time, and intangible flows of goods.

[20] Reavis Cox, Charles S. Goodman, and Thomas C. Fichandler, *Distribution in a High Level Economy* (Englewood Cliffs, N.J.: Prentice-Hall, Inc., 1965).

Movements of goods through space is rather a self-explanatory term and is probably the easiest of the three to identify. It refers to the actual physical handling of goods from the raw material stage right to the ultimate customer.

In the case of movement through time, the flow refers to the goods sitting still while time passes. Generally, the vast majority of goods remain stationary awaiting the time when someone will do something with them. This waiting, of course, involves storing, financing, and risk-taking on someone's part and is as much a part of the marketing process as the more obvious tasks.

The third flow concept is the rearranging of relations among goods and people in social space just as transportation rearranges locations in space or storage in time. At any instant, all goods are owned and all risks are borne by someone. Thus, a socially arranged and sanctioned pattern of relationships between goods and people is developed. Some examples of these intangible flows are the flow of ownership, the flow of negotiation, and the flow of information.

> These concepts of movement not only make possible measurement and counting, but they also make it easier for the student of marketing to describe what marketing does. Extraction and manufacturing are easily observable and often spectacular as physical operations; but marketing is largely intangible. Physical processes somehow seem to be only contributing to the essential business of getting goods ordered and sold. The heart of distribution is people writing and talking to each other as they arrange transactions, and this essential business is very difficult to observe. Reducing it to flows makes it both observable and measurable.[21]

RETAIL DISTRIBUTION

The retail network, including department stores, mail-order houses, chain stores, supermarkets, discount houses, voluntary group retailers, house-to-house sellers, and consumer cooperatives, is undergoing such significant changes that the term "retail revolution" has been used to describe the retail scene. The major elements in this revolution, or rapid evolution, are these:

> *New Consumer Needs.* Increased demand for services are reflected in the break-down of traditional merchandise classifications; more varied product mixes supplied by manufacturers.
>
> *New Shopping Habits.* These are reflected in changed consumption habits and life styles; suburban population movement is resulting in new store locations and hours—i.e., branch stores, night shopping; working wives with more money and less time to spend it; increase in family shopping.
>
> *Customer Orientation.* Stores managed as a customer-oriented dis-

tribution system and organized to serve customers' needs, not tradition.

Retail Concentration. Balance of power shifting from small to large, multimerchandise classification store; one hundred major retailers in U.S. account for 50 percent of total retail volume in their major merchandise classifications.

Shopping Centers. Growth from less than 50 shopping centers in 1946 to 12,000 in 1970, accounting for one-fifth of total retail sales (one-fourth, excluding automobile sales); effort to serve customers as they want, when and where they want, by offering a total shopping experience greater than the sum of the attractions of individual stores.

Discount Pricing. It has forced many adjustments and pricing innovations on conventional retailers and has changed attitudes of both retailers and consumers.

Self-Service. This type of service has expanded to nearly every form of retailing and is replacing personal selling in many stores.

Automatic Merchandising. It is a $3 billion industry covering a wide range of products; it reflects willingness of consumer to buy at any location.

Rental Selling. This applies to both products and services; consumers are more concerned with use than ownership.

Credit, Private Labels, New Products. Retail competition is growing more rigorous and widespread, as illustrated by the use of trading stamps, games, and special promotions.

WHOLESALE DISTRIBUTION

A wholesaler is a merchant middleman who sells to retailers and other resellers and/or to industrial, institutional, and commercial users.[22] Merchants who render all services normally expected in the wholesale trade are known as service wholesalers; those rendering only some of the wholesale services are known as limited-function wholesalers. The latter group is composed mainly of cash-and-carry wholesalers, who do not render credit or delivery service; drop-shipment wholesalers, who sell for delivery by the producer direct to the buyer; truck wholesalers, who combine selling, delivery, and collection in one operation; and mail-order wholesalers, who perform the selling service entirely by mail. The term *jobber* is used as a synonym for wholesaler.

Both wholesalers and retailers are described as merchant middlemen because they own the goods they sell. Agent middlemen do not own the goods for which they negotiate purchases or sales. The main types of agent middlemen are brokers, commission houses, manufacturers' agents, selling agents, factors, and auction companies.

[22] Surveys of wholesaling are T. N. Beckman, N. H. Engle, and R. D. Buzzell, *Wholesaling: Principles and Practice,* 3rd ed. (New York: The Ronald Press Company, 1959); Richard M. Hill, *Wholesaling Management: Text and Cases* (Homewood, Ill.: Richard D. Irwin, Inc., 1963); and David A. Revzan, *Wholesaling in Marketing Organization* (New York: John Wiley & Sons, Inc., 1961).

The decline of the wholesaler has been predicted for many years. Historically, manufacturers and retailers have been ready to "eliminate the middleman" for some time now, and the wholesaler has come to seem the most vulnerable of middlemen. He is able to survive because he can perform certain functions more economically or efficiently than others in the marketing channel. For retailers, other resellers, or industrial users, the wholesaler performs the following functions:

> Anticipates customer requirements;
> Assembles goods from a multitude of sources;
> Buys in economical quantities;
> Maintains a reservoir of goods;
> Delivers promptly;
> Grants credit;
> Provides informational and advisory services.

For manufacturers, the wholesaler:

> Establishes connections with the whole field of retail outlets;
> Furnishes advice as a distribution specialist;
> Reduces costs of physical distribution;
> Reduces manufacturer's capital requirements;
> Simplifies accounting and credit problems.[23]

The benefits of these middleman services to retailers, industrial users, and manufacturers remain important. Cox, Goodman, and Fichandler identify four categories of recent changes in wholesaling which contribute to its continued existence: (1) increasing specialization, (2) improvements in operating methods, (3) closer control of sales activity, and (4) closer cooperation with retailers.[24]

Wholesalers will continue to be an important part of the distribution scene. Manufacturers of products sold to large number of customers have the problem of determining whether "wholesale functions" can be best performed by independent middlemen or by the manufacturer's own distribution network.

[23] Herman C. Nolen, "The Modern Wholesaler and His Adjustment to a Changing Economy," in *Marketing in Progress: Patterns and Potentials*, ed., Hiram C. Barksdale (New York: Holt, Rinehart & Winston, Inc., 1964), p. 463.

[24] Cox *et al. Distribution in a High Level Economy*, p. 51.

8

INTEGRATING MARKETING IN ENVIRONMENTS OF UNCERTAINTY

The preceding chapters indicate the impact of accelerating scientific technological, and social change on marketing. The chapters emphasize that marketing and business will undergo accelerating change in a world of uncertainty as we enter "the third industrial revolution" and what may be a new stage of societal development. In this chapter, certain emerging developments are noted, and their relationship to the adaptive processes in marketing considered.

Each chapter of this book focuses on the consumer-citizen orientation, the conception and implementation of planning and profit goals, and other elements of the marketing concept as identified in Chapter 1. This final chapter focuses on aspects of a current management problem—the evolution of current corporate and managerial marketing concepts into new concepts of management appropriate for a transitional world society.

It was stated in Chapter 2 that the post-industrial society in the United States is evolving into a technetronic society. Throughout the book the following major characteristics of this new society are emphasized:

1. A new information technology characterized by rapid developments in computers and the application of quantitative techniques and behavioral analysis applied to marketing and business problems;
2. A social system-oriented view of business with a new framework for evaluating market information, particularly information communicated by marketing.

This chapter emphasizes the integration of information management and value changes as they affect marketing and business policy. Broader marketing applications in such areas as socio-marketing are discussed later in this chapter.

Historically, marketing has been looked upon as a narrow function relating primarily to exchange activities between individual consumers and businesses. Marketing, as a core area of business, is evolving into a relatively broad discipline involving all facets of consumer-firm interaction. It is becoming concerned with behavioral and functional processes, which are areas far removed from those of traditional marketing.

Integrating the Field of Marketing

One test of marketing's ability to survive and flourish in the future may be the ability to integrate and apply the metamarketing concepts identified throughout this book to the challenges posed by changes in business and society. Under the metamarketing view, the major task of marketing leadership is that of integrating all elements of an organization into an effective system that will profitably accomplish marketing goals. The integration of marketing is also essential to the assessment of marketing opportunity discussed in Chapter 3, the planning-organizational elements considered in Chapters 4 and 5, and to the management of the marketing-mix elements discussed in Chapters 6 and 7.

Robert Ferber discussed three ways in which marketing will become more integrated. First, "marketing functions will become more integrated with each other and with other functions of the business enterprise; second, there will be an integration of marketing theory with practice; and, third, a more unified approach will be taken with behavioral and quantitative techniques through the use of more realistic models of human behavior that will aid in problem solving."[1] These integrations, including greater social considerations, will certainly produce a marketing discipline and practice more congruent with our technologically based information society.

The managerial, scientific-technological, institutional, and societal-legal dimensions that compose the "new marketing" are each a part of the total field of marketing. By considering these four dimensions within a systems context, the integrations discussed by Ferber can be readily perceived. Yet most firms have not yet begun to manage all of these elements effectively. Despite the efforts of marketing managers, product or brand managers, committees, and training programs, to coordinate all the elements, integrated marketing still remains an elusive achievement.

MANAGERIAL INTEGRATION

The integration of marketing with other business functions has been a long-time problem. Sales, advertising, product planning, research and development, and marketing research have often been isolated functions with a specific orientation confined to solving narrowly defined problems. The recent realization that the firm actually operates as a systematized unit has resulted in greater value being placed on decision-makers capable

---

[1] Robert Ferber, "The Expanding Role of Marketing in the 1970s," *Journal of Marketing*, xxxiv, No. 1 (January 1970), 29.

of framing specific problems in terms of their over-all impact on the system. Such system sensitivity demands superior leadership to efficiently coordinate the knowledge and skills of new marketing specialists with the wisdom and experience of seasoned generalists.

Despite the remarkable success of modern business in solving identified problems, the fact remains that a major management task is one of problem identification and definition. This book has been designed to indicate methods of improving the decision-making process in marketing. Drucker has summarized this view in a statement which indicates that effective management results come from exploiting opportunities, not from solving problems:

> All one can hope to get by solving a problem is to restore normality. All one can hope, at best, is to eliminate a restriction on the capacity of the business to obtain results. The results themselves must come from the exploitation of opportunities. . . . The pertinent question is not how to do things right, but how to find the right things to do, and to concentrate resources and efforts on them.[2]

Changes reflected in the consumer-citizen value structure have given rise, not only to new marketing opportunities, but also to the restructuring of the managerial, scientific-technological, institutional, and societal-legal dimensions encompassed by the field of marketing. These changes are only a partial indication of the many new phenomena that will be witnessed by marketers during the next decade. Some of the more apparent changes in management of marketing will include the following:

1. The trend toward decentralization of authority within large firms will continue and probably accelerate.
2. A critical shortage of qualified marketing management will develop.
3. Top-level management will rely increasingly on formal corporate planning systems.
4. Companies will have to modify their selling method to meet the needs of large, diversified, multinational customers, both manufacturers and distributors.
5. There will be extensive experimentation in the definition of a proper role for corporate marketing units.[3]

The new and complex environment confronting the marketing executive will require a systems-oriented planning and organizing framework. Only through innovative management will the integration of scientific, institutional, and social knowledge inputs result in effective marketing action programs.

[2] Peter F. Drucker, *Managing for Results* (New York: Harper & Row, Publishers, 1964), p. 5.

[3] From Robert D. Buzzell, "What's Ahead for Marketing Managers?" *Journal of Marketing*, xxxiv, No. 1 (January 1970), 4–5.

SCIENTIFIC-TECHNOLOGICAL INTEGRATION

Modern marketing is the composite of a "new technology" blended with the concepts of established disciplines. Knowledge from the behavioral sciences, such as learning, cognitive, and personality theories, has been integrated with quantitative expertise to provide a better understanding of buyer behavior and the over-all interrelationship between the firm and the consumer-citizen.

The knowledge and information explosion has placed the marketing executive in a society commonly characterized by continuous and accelerated change. The time lapse between development and use of new knowledge is diminishing rapidly. Consequently, the time frame encompassing transformation of marketing philosophy and theory into general application has been considerably shortened. Changes in computer technology, the development of more sophisticated means to aid decision-making, and the greater acceptance of the university as a source of new knowledge all serve to radically alter the business community and society as a whole. The pace of accumulating and utilizing new knowledge shows no sign of slackening. The concept of information is rapidly becoming a dominant characteristic of this society and accordingly holds untold implications and opportunities for marketing executives of the future. Business firms and individual executives face a major problem in learning to cope with this change and in operating successfully in a world destined to be far different from the one we know.

Marketing, as well as other disciplines, has relied on the computer to provide the means necessary for the realization of many quantitative breakthroughs. Computer utilization in multivariate analysis is an example of the potential that exists for the advancement of marketing techniques.

> The role of the computer in furthering the maturity of the marketing discipline is thus immense. By diffusing multivariate methods, it is likely to enable marketing researchers to attempt large-scale marketing information systems in which an integrated marketing approach can be undertaken. It will enable researchers to test and estimate parameters of complex generalized theories and models. With the use of multivariate methods, the computer is likely to generate a sudden increase in in-depth scientific empirical research on well-known issues in marketing.[4]

Without the progressive development of computer hard- and software, the present level of operational efficiency and economic importance of analytical techniques would never have been achieved. The growth of computer utilization has marked the advent of firms specializing in the marketing of computer services. These companies, on either a time-shar-

---

[4] Jagdish N. Sheth, "The Multivariate Revolution in Marketing Research," *Journal of Marketing*, xxxv, No. 1 (January 1971), 19.

ing, leasing, or rental basis provide the equipment and/or technical expertise required to perform not only complex quantitative analyses, but also routine business functions such as billing, accounting, and inventory control. By renting the services of computer firms, smaller companies are able to obtain services that would otherwise not be available because of the large investments associated with computer installation and operation.

Perhaps more important than reliance on the computer is the significant trend toward education in and application of computer technology by marketing personnel within business as well as academic circles. A recent survey by Robert Kegerreis on the integration of marketing management and the computer has indicated that:

> Regardless of the mixed picture of computer usage, the trend is unmistakable. The use of computers will grow inexorably both in scope and rigor. Tomorrow's top marketing executive will have been trained in college in computer applications, will have a miniature desktop computer printer at his elbow with instant access to the data bases in his company, in his trade association, and in numerous public and private sources.[5]

INSTITUTIONAL INTEGRATION

Important changes in institutional structures have been realized through such phenomena as the growth of vertical marketing systems and inter-type competition, the polarity of retail trade, the acceleration of institutional life cycles, the emergence of the "free-form" corporation, and the expansion of non-store retailing.[6]

Changes in the institutional environment are important to the marketer, for they greatly influence the formulation and implementation of over-all marketing strategy. Rarely can large established institutions be readily molded to reflect current needs. Nevertheless, such adaptive efforts must be attempted if favorable competitive positions are to be maintained.

As outlined in Chapter 3, technology, population shifts, concentration of power in a few large companies, communication advances, internationalization of business and affluence, are all current forces underlying institutional shifts.

SOCIETAL INTEGRATION

The concept of the consumer-citizen has broadened the established theme that the "Customer is King." Environmental and social concerns have re-

---

[5] Robert J. Kegerreis, "Marketing Management and the Computer: An Overview of Conflict and Contract," *Journal of Marketing*, xxxv, No. 1 (January 1971), 3.

[6] William R. Davidson, "Changes in Distributive Institutions," *Journal of Marketin*, xxxiv, No. 1 (January 1970), 7.

cently begun to receive recognition as important dimensions to consumer service. There is a growing trend to balance the gains of individual consumer satisfaction against the social and environmental consequences. For example, auto emissions affect young citizens and non-automobile owners as well as those who own and operate automobiles; airplane noise and combustion affect the life styles of millions who seldom fly; insecticides and detergents affect almost all world citizens, including those of non-industrialized cultures. Growing recognition of such interactions is one thing society expects of the new high-level professional marketing manager charged with responsibility for societal management.[7]

Environmental Management and Socio-marketing

Environmental management is not a new concept embodied with specific models or operational techniques; it is more a philosophical reflection whose purpose it is to modify existing concepts by adding a new dimension to managerial problems. Environmental management is implemented by expanding the operational philosophy of decision-makers to encompass environmental criteria within the problem-solving framework.

As it grows in importance, environmental management will find itself becoming an increasingly critical input to the decision process of more and more organizational functions, especially in the formulation of marketing policy. The marketing concept sets the tone for corporate operations by lending structure and direction to the entire functional system. Therefore, observing the influence of environmental inputs on marketing operations makes it possible to determine their impact upon the total system. Corporate responsiveness to technological, social, and environmental forces will be primarily manifested by bold and imaginative implementations of the elements of the marketing mix discussed in Chapters 6 and 7.

For the most part, corporate social responsibility has been considered in the context of business obligation to society. Recently, however, marketing executives have begun to perceive a new dimension to social responsibility as it concerns environmental management and other areas—the dimension of opportunity. Marketers realize that there is more to be gained from social activism than the minimal placation of the general public and favorable public relations. The development of marketing programs based on socio-marketing promotional tactics is currently under exploration. Ford Motor Company developed a promotional campaign around a "We Listen Better" theme. Ford is responding to public opinion in areas such as auto-safety devices, pollution-control research, and highway safety. They also encourage consumers to write the Company about social and environmental problems *and* solutions which they, as the driving public, consider urgent. This "We Listen Better" theme operationalizes the con-

---

[7] For a discussion of ethics and environmental changes see Eugene J. Kelley, "Ethical Considerations for Scientifically Oriented Marketing Management," in *Science in Marketing Management,* M. S. Moyer, ed. (Toronto: York University, 1969), pp. 69–87.

sumerism philosophy by communicating the image that Ford is sincerely attempting to respond to social and environmental problems as perceived by consumers. The seventies may witness the maturity of socially sophisticated consumers, sensitive not only to their own needs but also to those of society. Social consciousness appears to be more than just a short-lived consumer fad and, as such, it warrants closer marketing attention.

In this era of rigorous competition marketers are continuously searching for effective and differentiable competitive strategies. Unfortunately, rising costs, increased government regulation, and the preliminary effects of overpopulation have, to varying degrees, constrained the traditional flexibility of the marketing mix. Under these circumstances, perhaps more firms will investigate the feasibility of "socio-marketing" tactics.

There is nothing esoteric about the socio-marketing concept; it simply entails incorporating socially responsive efforts into marketing programs. It adds another dimension to the concept of market segmentation by introducing social variables into the system. As with traditional concepts of market segmentation, specific promotional appeals are designed for and communicated to the identified target segments. Today one does not have to search very far to evidence manifestations of the trend toward consumer activism. Cesar Chavez and the California wine growers are acquainted with the power of the socially conscious consumer. The Chemical Bank of New York has recently launched a promotional campaign designed to market its newly conceived "Air Pollution Shares." The point to be made is that the list is growing and with it the possibilities for socio-marketing.

Another significant impetus to socio-marketing may be derived from government pressures. The current governmental strategy of maintaining a low profile on socially oriented programs through private enterprise is an important indication of what may come. Perhaps the future will witness such direct fiscal inducements as additional subsidies and tax exemptions or such indirect measures as tax exemption of dividends, interest, or capital gains income for the investors or creditors of socially desirable investments.

Marketing Audit

The marketing audit, a systematic and comprehensive appraisal of the total marketing operation, is used to appraise the extent of integration in a firm, the foundations underlying marketing operations, and a firm's understanding of newer marketing concepts. If properly executed, the audit can contribute to an appraisal and reintegration of all aspects of marketing.

> . . . the audit is a searching inquiry into the character and validity of the fundamental premises underlying a company's marketing operations. It is a review and evaluation of the assumptions, conceptions, and expectations that guide executives in their planning and operating decisions. It is a planned effort to test and assess executive beliefs and opinions about the character of the

market, the company's position in the market, the company's objectives and capabilities, and the effectiveness of the various policies, methods, personnel, and organization structures which are or might be employed.[8]

In auditing a marketing operation it is appropriate to evaluate the degree to which a firm is utilizing the contemporary marketing developments emphasized in this book. For example, an evaluation of a firm's competitive effectiveness would consider the organization's ability to innovate and adapt to marketing changes. Use of the new marketing concepts and analytical tools discussed provide a measure of enterprise effectiveness. Recent advances in marketing science and in the business applications of the behavioral sciences represent benefits of the interdisciplinary approach that are proving useful in the solution of marketing problems for some management groups.

Two major points to be evaluated are how the firm utilizes the marketing concept, and how it understands and analyzes the marketing environment. The entire business process is tested against its ability to develop, produce, and market products that satisfy consumer needs profitably. Marketing management's function under this concept is to mobilize a firm's total resources in order to capitalize on market opportunities by serving consumers wants and needs. The consumer-citizen is the focal point around which marketing and, ultimately, all competitive business activities revolve. The second point to be evaluated is the degree to which management understands and analyzes the environment in which the marketing effort will take place. Changes in the technological, social, economic, and political structure of society have profound marketing implications. In this changing environment, the resources of the company are programmed, organized, and controlled to achieve the goals set by management. The notion that marketing goals should be identified and an action program designed to achieve these goals is central to the marketing concept.

International Marketing

International marketing is becoming a most critical factor in the growth of modern business. In today's turbulent world, marketing may be one means of facilitating economic solutions to problems with which military or political efforts have failed. "World peace through world trade" may yet become more than a corporate slogan. One manifestation of the superiority of economic approaches to military and political approaches is the liberalization of east-west trade and its effect on the political structures of the Communist world. Marketing's role in the developing countries is yet another frontier.

International marketing provides a means, not only of redistributing "economic prosperity," but also of generating it through the tapping of

[8] Abraham Schuchman, *The Marketing Audit: Its Nature, Purposes, and Problems*, American Management Association Report #32, 1959, p. 12.

potential markets. The very fact that many international markets still remain dormant indicates new and imaginative marketing strategies must continue to be formulated and operationalized. An indication of the success of such strategies is ". . . the emergence of corporations of unprecedented size, complexity, breadth, and international scope. For example:

- In 1969, International Business Machines Corporation had total sales of $7.2 billion with $2.5 billion coming from outside the U.S. This company operated in 108 countries with 99,000 foreign employees, one-third of the company's total payroll.
- The International Telephone and Telegraph Corporation had worldwide sales of over $5.4 billion from 200 companies and divisions in 67 countries employing a total of 300,000 persons. It derived 40% of its sales and a substantial share of its $300,000,000 before-tax income from assets outside the U.S." [9]

These strategies must reflect the peculiarities of the particular market environment and must not be unduly influenced by experiences in the domestic market. As David Leighton has pointed out, ". . . the old world of trade has been largely superseded by the multinational corporation and direct investment." [10] He sees this as central to marketing internationally in the 1970s. The economic development of the modern world has resulted in competition from nations geographically and culturally compatible with what were once American-dominated markets. Nevertheless, international marketing not only continues to hold out a promising financial opportunity to American business, but it also provides the American public with a means for communication of its cultural values in a rapidly growing world.

Broadening Market Applications

William Lazer wrote that "Marketing is not an end in itself. It is not the exclusive province of business management. Marketing must serve not only business but also the goals of society. It must act in concert with broad public interest." [11] This theme suggests more than being socially oriented; it suggests that marketing principles and talents can be applied to a broad range of social problems. Philip Kotler and Sidney J. Levy extend the marketing concept to include marketing and marketing management in non-business, non-profit organizations.[12] These elements—service to societal goals and non-business marketing—extend marketing beyond

[9] David S. R. Leighton, "The Internationalization of American Business— The Third Industrial Revolution," *Journal of Marketing*, xxxiv, No. 3 (July 1970), 3.

[10] *Ibid.*, p. 6.

[11] William Lazer, "Marketing's Changing Social Relationship," *Journal of Marketing*, xxxiii, No. 1 (January 1969), 3.

[12] Philip Kotler and Sidney J. Levy, "Broadening the Concept of Marketing," *Journal of Marketing*, xxxiii, No. 1 (January 1969), 10–15.

the traditional boundaries of the firm to include all want and need satisfactions of the customer-citizen.

The broadening concept of marketing is further supported by the fact
that a "product" can take many forms—physical, intangible services, persons, organizations, or ideas.[13] Government—local, state, and national—and
non-profit organizations have assumed the role of providing many of these
products; in this function they assume the role of producing want and
need satisfaction. Marketing concepts can be extended to meet the challenges of these non-profit organizations in such areas as marketing health
services and family planning.

Professionalism and Marketing Education

In traditional terms marketing cannot be classified as a profession.
For example, it does not require entrance examinations, nor does it govern
the action of its members through licensing requirements and a central
organization. However, many contemporary marketers are evolving into
true professionals. Although they are not required to be so by regulation,
today's marketing executives are highly skilled specialists who fully utilize
an interdisciplinary approach to managerial problem-solving. The modern marketing executive integrates inputs from the behavioral sciences,
the physical sciences, and other disciplines into marketing strategies in
order to achieve corporate objectives.

There have also emerged organizations, such as the American Marketing Association, that provide structure and direction to the field. To a
lesser extent, the regulatory or ethical aspects of the field are also formally
or informally influenced by these organizations.

Although specialization normally connotes a narrow perspective, the
effective modern marketing professional is one who reflects the dynamic
changes in the business world in the implementation of his marketing
skills. This responsiveness must not result in a preoccupation with the
justification of marketing policy to critical groups in government and society. A two-way flow of communications is necessary. While the objectives and limitations of business operations should be thoroughly explained
to the public, it is equally important that the demands of interested groups
—the labor force, consumers, government, and concerned citizens—be
recognized and transmitted to management for evaluation in order to be
incorporated into the decision framework. Tomorrow's marketing professional will not only be a highly competent and technical practitioner, but
also capable of effectively ordering socio-environmental priorities from a
systems perspective.

These same challenges are also facing marketing educators and students. Social responsibility is emerging as a highly significant factor in
both business management and business education. The issues are important in terms of projecting a favorable public image, but more fundamentally in formulating and implementing corporate policies on a wide variety

---

[13] *Ibid.*, pp. 10–12.

of issues where the public interest is seen at stake. Therefore, marketers must be capable of understanding and developing strategies which reflect a broad range of environmental concerns and social attitudes in order to be able to operate competently in this new environment.

Development of highly specific marketing techniques must be concurrently complemented with a satisfactory general knowledge of the most current management practice. "Attention must be directed at educating marketing generalists to complement the current emphasis on educating marketing specialists and technicians." [14] Much of the detailed knowledge regarding organizational structures and procedures will come from actual experience, but the learning process is greatly facilitated if a general appreciation of management fundamentals exists.

The integration of marketing practice, new information technology, and social responsibility considerations, will be the most important problems facing management and management educators during the 1970s. The required changes in the value structure of business and industry are suggested in an article by Gelb and Brien, who state that the survival of mankind is a theme for higher education.[15] Management actions in the future may be tested in terms of their effect on man's survival.

The marketing graduate of twenty-five years ago learned, basically, to sell soap at a time when marketing was essentially considered to be the business of buying and selling. In recent years, marketing graduates have learned not only to sell soap, but also to understand computer analyses of the soap market. Both the aspects of sales and market analysis are included in most curricula today. In addition, marketing students today are learning to evaluate the effects of that "soap" not only on individual consumers, but also on society as a whole. Current emphasis is on a cost-benefit analysis of the massive resources committed to the commercial success of soap or other products. The criteria goes beyond the traditional income statement.[16]

The knowledge and skills necessary to be a professional marketer cannot be developed within a short academic period. Achievement of marketing professionalism is a life-long process that transcends past experience and generates itself through a lasting commitment to learning and self-development. The nature and extent of the commitment required will be largely influenced by the forces and issues described here and in other books of the Foundations of Marketing Series; however, the effectiveness of this commitment depends upon the individual's effort. In the last analysis, professional development in marketing is largely a matter of self-development.

Any reader who considers himself a member, or an aspiring member, of the professional marketing community should continuously undertake a

[14] William Lazer, "Marketing Education: Commitments for the 1970s," *Journal of Marketing*, xxxiv, No. 3 (July 1970), 10.

[15] Betsy D. Gelb and Richard H. Brien, "Survival and Social Responsibility: Themes for Marketing Education and Management," *Journal of Marketing*, xxxv, No. 2 (April 1971), 3.

[16] *Ibid.*

critical self-analysis and a systematic personal audit covering such questions as:

- Can I meet the challenge of the new technology and a new set of societal values?
- Do I comprehend the implications of environmental change as it presents marketing and social opportunities?
- Can I redefine my personal and business objectives in terms broad enough to reflect current and developing marketing opportunities and realities?
- Can I develop creative and innovative programs reflecting a distinctive corporate competence to serve the basic market areas of the firm?
- Can I, through managerial or individual contribution, develop the human and knowledge resources of an organizational system to capitalize on new needs and opportunities?
- Can I account for my performance in terms of professional ethical standards, and do I have the courage to challenge those who cannot?

These are but a few of the questions that must be answered if the pursuit of learning is to result in continuous "self renewal" and personal growth. In the final analysis, the stature of marketing and the individual contributions of marketers is founded on how effectively each of us answers these questions.

INDEX

INDEX

A

Aaker, David A., 47
Advertising (see Promotion policy)
Advertising research, 107, 108
Affluence, 38, 39
American Marketing Association (AMA), 124
American Medical Association, 47
American Motors Corporation, 85
American Telephone and Telegraph Company (AT&T), 17, 38
Association of National Advertisers, 107
Attitude, 46

B

Behavioral analysis, 45, 49
Berensen, Conrad, 78
Boeing Corporation (see SST), 21, 37
Borch, Frederick J., 23
Boulding, Kenneth E., 65
Brien, R., 125
Bristol-Myers Company, 42
Brzezinski, Zbighiew, 19
Business:
   definition, 6
   orientation, 14
Buyer behavior (see Consumer, behavior)

C

Caterpillar Tractor Company, 42, 45
Change:
   environmental, 4, 6, 25, 38, 71, 123
   institutional, 19, 41, 119
   managing, 15, 16, 19, 70, 84, 117

Change (Cont.)
   technological, 38
Channels of distribution:
   definition, 110
   retail, 41, 90
   wholesale, 113
Chavez, Caesar, 121
Chemical Bank of New York, 121
Common Market (EEC), 10, 42
Communication:
   analysis, 86, 98, 100
   channels, 98, 100
   components, 98
   feedback, 100
   mix, 86, 99
   process, 99
   types, 100, 124
Competition, 7, 42, 92
Competitive policy, 5, 92
Computer marketing, 43
Computer technology, 30, 48, 118
Consumer:
   behavior, 24, 43, 45
   satisfaction, 1, 8, 12, 15, 16, 22, 29, 79
Consumer-citizen, 2, 15, 117, 119
Consumerism, 47
Control:
   financial, 34
   management, 34, 74, 77
Corporate:
   mission, 15, 54, 55, 59
   resources, 83
   self-concept, 55
Cox, Reavis, 111
Customer:
   demand, 92
   orientation, 35, 57, 69
   service, 90

D

Davidson, William R., 41
Day, George S., 47
Dean, Joel, 93
Decision-making:
  buyer, 25
  managerial, 117
  tools, 27, 30
Decision sciences, 27
Demographic analysis, 44, 49
Distribution:
  channels, 110
  flows, 111
  models, 109
  retail, 41, 90, 112
  wholesale, 113
Drucker, Peter F., 3, 4, 117
du Pont de Nemours & Company, 38

E

Entrepreneurial functions, 33
Environmental change, 4, 6, 25, 38, 71
Environmental forces, 16, 26, 38, 39, 75
  consumer, 15, 43
  economic and political, 39
  societal, 46
  technological and scientific, 43
Environmental management, 64, 75, 120
Ethics, 13
Exchange function, 3

F

Fayol, Henri, 53
Ferber, Robert, 116
Fichlandler, Thomas C., 111
Ford Motor Company, 81, 95, 120
Free-form corporation, 119
Fuller Brush Company, 110
Furthering concept, 14
Futurism, 39

G

Galbraith, John K., 40
Gelb, Betsy D., 125
General Electric Company, 48, 53, 110
General Foods Corporation, 81
General Learning Corporation, 48
General Motors Corporation, 17
Gillette Company, 95
Goals:
  corporate, 15, 52, 54, 57, 59
  definition, 57
Goodman, Charles S., 111
Governmental control, 38
Grand strategy, 59, 60

Gross National Product (GNP), 40

H

Howard, John A., 25, 45, 49
Human behavior (see Consumer, behavior)

I

Information management, 20, 29, 115, 118
Information society, 20
Information system:
  definition, 30
  marketing, 15, 29, 78
Information technology, 16, 20, 28, 107, 115
Innovation:
  definition, 61
  management of, 61, 79
  process, 61, 63
  product, 15, 61, 63
  technological, 27
Institutional life cycle, 119
International Business Machines Corporation (IBM), 6, 7, 81, 83, 91, 123
International marketing, 9, 122
International Telephone and Telegraph Corporation (IT&T), 123

J

J. C. Penney Company, 41
J. L. Hudson Company, 64
Jobber, 113
Joint Economic Committee, 10

K

Kappel, Frederick, 17
Kegerreis, Robert J., 119
Kennedy, John F., 96
Knowledge explosion, 21, 118
Kotler, Philip, 14, 31, 45, 93, 123

L

Lazer, William, 25, 123
Leadership:
  creative, 75
  marketing, 34, 75
Leighton, David S. R., 123
Levitt, Theodore, 35, 48, 97, 102
Levy, Sidney J., 14, 123
Life cycle:
  consumer, 44
  institutional, 41
  product, 83, 86

Life style:
changes, 38
definition, 25
influences on, 3
Ling-Temco-Vought, Incorporated (LTV), 37
Luck, David J., 82

M

Market offering, 80
Market segmentation, 49
Market share, 92
Marketing:
as a discipline, 10
control, 77
definition, 3
education, 124
field, 2, 116
institutional integration, 119
knowledge areas, 23
major approaches to study, 1, 2, 11, 116, 117
classic institutional approach, 11
managerial approach, 13
scientific-technological approach, 13
social approach, 3, 13
managerial integration, 116
orientation, 65
orientations to:
legalistic orientation, 3, 9
political orientation, 9
social system orientation, 3, 9, 54, 115
professionalism, 124
scientific-technological integration, 118
societal integration, 119
the systems approach to, 17, 28, 34
transaction, 3, 101
Marketing audit, 34, 121
Marketing company, 72, 74
Marketing concept, 10, 15, 16, 29, 52, 54, 72, 101, 120
Marketing effort:
evaluation and adjustment, 34, 77
managerial control, 15, 34, 74
organization and leadership, 34, 75
planning and programming, 33, 76
Marketing equation, 108
Marketing functions:
dual-core, 22
macro-, 13
micro-, 13
social, 8
Marketing intelligence, 15
Marketing management, 7, 9, 12, 14, 19, 22, 25, 120
Marketing mix, 33, 80
Marketing models, 78-79

Marketing myopia, 35
Marketing opportunity assessment, 16, 32, 35, 37, 38, 40, 61, 117
Marketing organizations, 65
Marketing planning:
as an enterprise function, 53, 106
as an entrepreneurial function, 33
long-range, 15, 53
overview, 5
social system orientation, 54
trends in, 54, 64
Marketing problems, 3, 15, 17, 70
Marketing research, 15, 106
Marketing systems:
components, 18
vertical integration of, 41
McColough, C. Peter, 7
McLuhan, Marshall, 102
Metamarketing approach, 11, 13, 20, 116
Minnesota Mining & Manufacturing Company (3M), 6
Mission:
corporate, 15, 54, 59
definition, 55
Moore, David G., 74

N

Nader, Ralph, 90
New marketing, 1, 116
New product innovation, 87, 89
Non-store retailing, 119

O

Objectives:
corporate, 15, 52, 54, 58, 59, 71, 92
definition, 58
Organization:
change, 65, 73
charts, 66, 69
control, 65
systems approach to, 29, 73

P

Packaging, 89
Packard, Vance, 90
Pillsbury, Charles A., 71
Pillsbury Company, 71
Planning:
horizon, 53
importance, 15, 64
process, 28, 52, 57
Price determination policies:
competition orientation, 94
cost orientation, 94
demand orientation, 94

Pricing:
    legal influences, 92, 109
    new products, 93, 95
    objectives, 95
    social influences, 93
    technological influences, 92
Problem solving, 105, 116
Product:
    definition, 124
    development, 16, 87
    differentiation, 90
    image, 80, 102
    life support, 88
    line, 86
    management, 82
    mix, 86
    planning, 16
    policy, 81
Production orientation, 35, 57, 71
Profit concept, 8, 16, 23, 58
Programmed Evaluation Review Technique (PERT), 30
Promotion:
    evaluation, 31, 107
    management, 101
    objectives, 103, 104
Promotion policy:
    advertising, 90, 98, 101, 103, 106
    personal selling, 103, 104
Public relations, 101
Purchasing power, 86

R

Ramond, Charles K., 107
Realsilk Hosiery Company, 110
Retail revolution, 112
Roosevelt, Franklin D., 9

S

Sales administration, 105
Sales force management, 105
Sales orientation, 71
Scarcity, 39
Scientific Data Systems Incorporated, 7
Sears, Roebuck and Company, 41
Selling process, 103
Servan-Schreiber, J. J., 9, 10
Sheth, Jadish N., 25

Singer Corporation, 45
Social class, 46
Social responsibility, 8, 47, 124
Societal management, 120
Socio-marketing, 120
Strategy:
    corporate, 42, 80
    definition, 58, 59
    pricing, 95
    product, 87
Supersonic transport (SST), 21
Systems:
    definition, 18
    environmental, 19
    marketing, 18, 29
    planning, 30, 117
Systems approach, 17, 28, 34

T

Tactics, 59
Technetronic society, 19, 115
Tilles, Seymour, 60
Time, Incorporated, 48
Toffler, Alvin, 19
Townsend, Robert, 8, 30, 58

U

Unilever, Limited, 45
Upjohn Pharmaceutical Company, 96
U.S. Steel Corporation, 53, 96

V

Volkswagenwerk, A. G., 80
Volume concept, 23

W

Whirlpool Corporation, 87

X

Xerox Corporation, 7

Y

Youth market, 51